LEADERSHIP

REVOLUTION

LORI MAZAN

PRESIDENT AND CHIEF COACHING OFFICER,
SOUNDING BOARD, INC.

LEADERSHIP

THE
FUTURE OF
DEVELOPING
DYNAMIC
LEADERS

REVOLUTION

WILEY

For general information on our other products and services or for technical support, please contact our Customer Care Department within the United States at (800) 762-2974, outside the United States at (317) 572-3993 or fax (317) 572-4002.

Wiley also publishes its books in a variety of electronic formats. Some content that appears in print may not be available in electronic formats. For more information about Wiley products, visit our web site at www.wiley.com.

Library of Congress Cataloging-in-Publication Data is Available:

ISBN 9781394171828 (cloth)
ISBN 9781394171842 (ePub)
ISBN 9781394171835 (ePDF)

Cover Design: Wiley
Cover Image: © Olha Huro/Getty Images

SKY10053052_081023

To my son Mike and his generation of present and future leaders.

Contents

Foreword

I never found leadership literature to be all that helpful. Throughout my career as an eager, ambitious leader, I often googled and read leadership books, articles, and how-tos as I encountered various leadership challenges. Although I got great frameworks and tips, it was hard to translate them into the situation in front of me.

So it's ironic that I'm now writing this Foreword for "yet another" leadership book. What I hope you will realize is that this is *not* just a leadership book. It has all the elements of a great leadership book—strong perspectives, innovative ideas, and, of course, incredible stories. But it's so much more. This isn't a how-to. It's a systematic breakdown of the process of aligning the individual values, belief systems, and mindsets that we all carry into the organizations that we work with throughout our careers. Lori's guidance is not just theoretical; it is an approach grounded in real-world experiences, offering practical tools and actionable insights that will undoubtedly transform the way you lead. And you'll be able to apply it again and again as you find yourself faced with new challenges.

I got to experience this process firsthand when Lori became my coach. My work with her transformed who am I as a leader and a person—so much so that I decided we needed to start a company together to scale this experience to thousands. I've

shared the origin story of Sounding Board with many people—
how Lori helped me uplevel a business to hundreds of millions in
revenue, and navigate the challenges as a young executive at a
high-growth startup. But what I haven't shared is that I was actually a reluctant skeptic. I didn't believe that I needed any help—
after all, I had been one of the youngest, fastest-promoted
executives. Didn't that prove I knew what I was doing?

What I've learned, and what I hope you'll learn, from this
book is that while it may be easier to keep doing what we know
and going it alone, there is another level you can unlock in your
life, particularly your professional career, if you don't. Everyone
needs a sounding board. Through the lens of dynamic development and the Leadership Revolution, Lori will challenge you
to become more self-aware, think about the "third option," and
cultivate a dynamic mindset that will equip you to take that "big
leap" in our ever-evolving world.

Lori, thank you for everything. You've been an incredible
coach and partner for me on our vision to build the world's most
impactful leaders. I'm so excited for you to share your approach
with the world, and help millions of leaders find their own
"green suit."

Christine Tao
CEO and Co-Founder, Sounding Board, Inc.

Preface

In my years in leadership development—first in traditional corporate training, then as an early practitioner in the emerging field of leadership coaching, and ultimately as an entrepreneur working to make leadership coaching accessible at much greater scale—I've seen and experienced a lot of change.

And I've encouraged change, too. Today's work world is so different from the one I started in that it requires an entirely different and much more dynamic mindset to succeed. If you try to develop leaders the way it was done 30 years ago, you won't get far.

Everyone knows this. But to a shocking degree, many organizations and managers stick to old assumptions and practices. Maybe most of all, they still assume that there is some single answer or set of answers that will work for every developing leader, in every context. It's an almost industrial-era mindset that's completely out of sync with the modern world. Yet it stubbornly hangs on.

But part of what drew me to coaching in the first place was the realization that this isn't true. An effective coach doesn't tell you what to do. Rather, an effective coach functions as a sounding board, or what I sometimes call a thinking partner, who helps you *decide* what to do, based on your context, by offering fresh and often challenging perspectives. An effective coach is not focused on procedure or applying the same leadership approach to every client. An effective coach is focused on outcome and results that coachees arrive at in their own way.

There's an art to this, as you'll see in the pages ahead, but for now just know that it goes beyond a one-size-fits-all methodology following prescribed steps in a certain order. By design, this approach is much more fluid—almost a conversation of thinking.

This willfully flexible, responsive approach is exactly why coaching has proven so effective. For years, top executives knew that effectiveness, because they were the only ones with access to it. But that's changing. In fact, that's the change I'm encouraging, through my career and, now, through this book.

The Spirit of a Coaching Engagement

There is most certainly a tried and tested methodology guiding the arc of a successful coaching engagement—and I've built this book to reflect and echo that arc. Think of the 12 chapters as 12 coaching sessions, each building on the last.

To help capture that flavor, each chapter/session begins with a snippet of coach–coachee dialogue that sets up what's about to be explored. And each ends with a set of provocative suggestions for further exploration. That reflects the way I conclude a session in real life: We cover a lot of territory, but it needs to end with what *you* make of it, discussing what's sticking, how it's shaping your point of view, what you are going to do about it.

This may sound like an untraditional approach for a book—but that's the point. I wrote this book because it is time to break with the old assumption that what works for one emerging leader works for all emerging leaders. We can't keep doing things the way they've "always" been done in an environment that has not only radically changed but that will keep on changing. What we need is not another prefab set of supposedly universal "rules," but, rather, the nimbleness and openness to respond to an environment in which the rules are changing all the time.

That's why this book is intentionally shaped so that it speaks to, and can be read from, multiple perspectives. Ideas about this new thinking on leadership development are examined, and their implications and opportunities explored, from several angles: a coach's point of view, an employee's point of view, and an organizational point of view.

Depending on who you are, where you are in your career, and what your context is, this book will—like a good coaching cycle—engage you in different ways. I hope you'll embrace that. What we're offering here is not a presentation; it's an informed and challenging *conversation*. That's where leadership development is headed, and there's no turning back.

> *This book is intentionally shaped so that it speaks to, and can be read from, multiple perspectives.*

Coaching is not only about doing, and it's definitely not about following a universal series of steps. Certainly coaching is focused on results and outcomes, but it's also about helping people to increase self-awareness, as well as coaxing them into new ways of thinking, all the while modeling how to deal with the unknown, with ambiguity, with the undeveloped space that leads to innovative thinking. In this book, sometimes I am telling and explaining, sometimes I am coaxing, and sometimes I am just helping people get comfortable with an unpredictable world. It's a balance, because this is not a self-help book. Yet sometimes I can offer ideas that can help people help themselves.

In that spirit, I'll sketch where we're headed from here.

What's Ahead

A productive coaching engagement starts with identifying the Big Leap that the coachee wants—or perhaps needs—to make. This is counterintuitive to some, who expect things to start with a lot of delving into what got the leader to this point. But it's actually better to focus on the future, and set the stakes, right away. Often, coachees are taken aback at the immediate challenge. And that's the idea.

Getting clarity on the Big Leap is a vital step, but of course it's only the first step. It's seldom, if ever, possible to offer a specific roadmap for the arc of a coaching engagement, but the rest of Part I of the book follows the theme of this chapter: figuring out how to make a Big Leap that is personalized to the individual and uniquely theirs, and still appropriate to the twenty-first-century workplace.

So, far starters: Out with the old. Breaking out of old patterns is always key to real change, so we'll delve into what that means for cultivating leaders at all levels, whether at big, established firms, or brand-new start-ups. Too much management practice today is based on thinking developed as far back as the 1950s. It's time to figure out what to hang on to—and what to discard.

The next step is to confront an eternal theme that's often ignored: Chances are, what you are doing now isn't creating what you want. That's why you—whether you're in HR, a manager, a CEO, a coachee, or a coach—need to focus on sorting out what you want. What you really, really want. And that may well mean embracing unpredictability and ambiguity.

This means learning to deal with resistance: from your organization or from yourself. Everyone is familiar with the feeling (or the colleague's excuse that "This always worked for me before" or "I don't know what else to do!"). The key is breaking through to new ways of thinking, and one framework for doing so is learning the difference between horizontal and vertical development models. You'll learn why to seek community—not "family." And you'll see why what matters is alignment—not uniformity.

The book's second section echoes the middle sessions of a coaching engagement: a crucial period, when the coachee can fall into the trap of feeling they've made changes, but most of those changes are (so far) superficial. It's in these sessions that the engagement must deepen, recommitting to a true Big Leap.

This flows directly into cycles of new actions and new behaviors that result in real impact and real growth. The specifics depend on understanding the culture and context in which you're operating (one size does not fit all!), and by learning to differentiate among diverse possibilities, you'll learn how to focus on (and achieve) real payoffs.

These middle sessions of a coaching engagement—and the middle chapters of this book—face down the real challenges of making true progress. This includes learning to confront and to break down failures and faulty steps. For individuals and organizations alike, taking novel steps and actions is risky, but that's okay: While difficult and messy, it's the only way to find the answers that lead to real progress. And as the coachee gets comfortable with this new way of thinking, breakthroughs follow.

For organizations, this can entail a similar embrace of new thinking around how leaders are developed and evaluated. It means less emphasis on the safe and familiar practice of cultivating "skills," and the more challenging practice of cultivating the leadership "capacity" for coping with the unpredictable (which is central to effective leadership). The middle sessions of a coaching engagement involve facing hard truths about making genuine change. But there are no easy shortcuts to real progress, and eventually that sinks in.

The book's third section reflects the home stretch of the cycle: As the pieces fall into place, the engagement becomes more and more forward-looking, building momentum toward a fresh mindset. Similarly, the last chapters address how our company, Sounding Board, is making the coaching-led development practice that has previously been accessible only to top executives much more available to a wider swath of management and aspiring leadership. Along the way, we've built our own systems for assessing and tracking leadership progress—methods that truly reflect the modern work dynamic in all its complexity, variety, and ambiguity.

Naturally a successful coaching cycle concludes with a well-earned sense of celebration. But it also involves a question: Now what? The goal is to be ever forward-looking, but also to leave the coachee with a sense of having attained a set of vital capabilities. A good coach fosters a sense of independence. The idea is: You've made a big leap—now keep going!

So what about *your* big leap? That's where we start: You have to accept that there is no single, works-for-everybody, five-check-points leadership paradigm. If you realize that the whole idea of leadership being one specific thing is simply a comforting myth, then you're ready to take the big leap into figuring out what works best for your company, your managers, your team, for you. Like a successful coaching relationship, this will take some work. But in the end, you'll find a new beginning.

Clarity

The Big Leap

I guess you'll need me to tell you a lot about my background.

Coach: Actually, we won't need to dwell too much on the past.

Then where should we begin?

Coach: Let's focus on what you really care about: your future.

Let's start with a big leap.

That's how a winning coaching relationship begins, not (contrary to common assumption) with a slow, meticulous excavation of the past, but with a clear, even blunt articulation of aspirations and goals. What are we trying to do here? What change do we wish, or *need*, to achieve?

In the case of this book, we need to start with a leap beyond the familiar "leadership" paradigm. At various points in my career I've been pressured to define a leadership philosophy that outlines "this is what it is to be a good leader." But I have remained adamant that I am not—and my company is not—going to do that. That's because (here's the big leap) there is no single leadership paradigm. We need to start by breaking the myth that being a leader means one specific thing.

For some reason, people resist this idea. So much leadership thinking dating back to the 1980s, 1990s, and early 2000s literally argues that to be a successful leader you must follow some very specific model: You have to be a leader *like this*. And then they'll proceed to name, say, five particular traits. I have read dozens of books like this—and I thought every one of them was wrong.

Not just wrong, but disappointing. Often my clients would say, "Oh, I read this book, and people are saying this is what successful leaders look like, so I want to have these five traits, too," but those traits didn't match with who they were as a person at all.

4

For example, I remember one client, a very analytical type, really rational and deliberate. He'd been quite successful. But then he'd read in some leadership book that was trendy at the time that leaders must be "charismatic." And he was pretty introverted. So he tried to *become* charismatic, and soon people who worked with him began asking, "What's wrong? Why are you acting like this?" It was all so out of character that some of his colleagues wondered if he was ok. That's one of the reasons he ended up seeking a coach—me. He explained how he'd read that he had to be charismatic. As with other clients who have tried to follow some supposedly universal success blueprint, I'd say, "Ah, well, to do that, you're going to become a totally different person."

And of course that's not sustainable. Because under stress, people default back to who they are. A leader is not going to be able to maintain a leadership façade that doesn't match who they are for very long, so why waste time trying to fit in someone else's mold? Let's find the style of leadership that matches who you really are as a leader, and that is also successful and influential and impactful. This will be an approach that a leader can sustain over time, because it fits their natural way of being. (That charisma-seeking client was relieved he could stop devoting all this energy to trying to become a different person. He

> *The best leaders are the people who can blend their authentic self with a set of skills, capabilities, and capacities.*

was already successful in his own style, and we just needed to focus on enhancing that success, mostly through improving his communication skills and habits, but in the context of his natural way of being.)

To be clear, this doesn't just mean "be yourself, period." After many years of "five traits" style advice, some of the leadership literature swung the other way with the concept of "authentic leadership." This approach suggests that to be successful you should be *only* "who you are"—be purely authentic at all times. This doesn't work, either. I might strike a strict tone at home, or give my kids the hairy eyeball, but that wouldn't be appropriate with a direct report. I once ran a training course for an oil company where one manager in the group kept making double entendre jokes about "horizontal drilling." I'm sure he was being his authentic "funny" self, but obviously you shouldn't be telling those kinds of jokes at work. Good leaders can't just blurt out anything that comes into their mind! They need to have skills, and use and think about them strategically. The best leaders are the people who can blend their authentic self with a set of skills, capabilities, and capacities.

The Unity of Opposites

So how do you find the place in the middle, blending who you naturally are with the skills and capabilities you need? It's elusive, to say the least. Just naming five traits is so much easier than trying to identify where the self and leadership interconnect. I've practiced Tai Chi Chuan for three decades, and one of its ideas that I use constantly is called " the unity of the opposites."

Just naming five traits is so much easier than trying to identify where the self and leadership interconnect.

This does *not* mean compromise. Most people think when you're trying to deal with dichotomies, you have to somehow compromise or come down in the middle. But the unity of opposites is more of a blend. In this case that means blending what makes good leaders—including appropriate traits for you—with who you naturally and authentically are. This is the magic formula.

It's not a compromise, because you are still being yourself, but in a leadership role. Think of it as your authentic self, wrapped in clothing of your role. That clothing has to fit not only your body but also with your style. Back in the 1950s and 1960s: Men wore a similar corporate uniform, right? Black suit, white shirt, and so on.

My dad had those suits, too, but he quietly refused to *only* wear that. I remember him wearing a green suit sometimes, and I'm sure he was the only guy in the office wearing a green suit. He first wore it on St. Patrick's Day. After that subtle change, he began wearing it as part of his regular rotation. He still wore his black and white to the big meetings but softly added a little of his own style into the mix. One of the big differences between the previous century and this century is that people now want to be themselves at work. In the past, maybe people wanted to be told how to "dress for success." Now everyone would just laugh at that. "You can't tell me how to dress!" they say. This more independent willingness to be yourself is a part of a new way of being at work.

Maybe the pendulum has swung a little too far, now that it's gone from "wear a black suit and a white shirt" all the way over to "wearing your pajamas on Zoom is fine." The point is, my dad wore those black suits when he needed to. But then other times, he just wore something else. He was able to blend.

The key, then, is not being the same person all the time, or showing the exact same behavior (or wearing the exact same clothes). It's ensuring that your behavior is in alignment with who you are—even at work, even in the context of your leadership.

The idea of trying to emulate five certain traits is the opposite of finding that blend. Those books and

It's ensuring that your behavior is in alignment with who you are—even at work, even in the context of your leadership.

theories are too one-size-fits-all, not allowing individuality or style differences, trying to force everyone into a black suit. The goal is to be secure in who you are and build from there. That's why what coaching does is the exact opposite of exploiting insecurities. It's about getting people comfortable with who they are, what their unique gifts are, and what their individual points of view are. It's about owning their personal experience and specific expertise and cultivating the ability to take the risk to show who they are—but still in the context of their leadership. It's about helping them, so to speak, find their perfect green suit.

Coaching's "Secret Weapon" Era

I've been an executive coach since the early 1990s—pretty much the beginning of the coaching industry—and it has turned out to be an interesting profession. In that time, two things happened. First, the coaching business itself has dramatically changed. And second, the process for developing leaders has changed, and is still changing.

In its early days, the practice of coaching was defined pretty narrowly. Originally associated with management-professor-turned-coach Marshall Goldsmith, the practice was first seen as a process for helping "derailed" executives get back on track. (This term refers to executives with a successful track record, but whose progress had stopped short of their perceived potential.) At that time, coaching was a "behind closed doors" activity: Executives didn't want anyone to know they had a coach! Sometimes a leader would even make a deal with a coach on the side, without the company knowing. In my own early days, I sometimes had contracts with leaders drawn from their discretionary budget. For some, it became almost like a secret weapon. No one wanted to be seen as "derailed," yet many saw the value of having a coach, much like an elite athlete.

Over time, HR departments got involved and a more formal process of coaching began. But there was not much oversight or clarity in reporting results, problems that in some ways still exist and that I'll address in the pages ahead. And while it was no longer such a secret activity, coaching was still widely seen as something only for the C-suite.

That's finally changing—as it should. Coaching tuned to follow the specific needs of an organization, and the individuality of the coachee, can be useful for all layers of management, and for closing all sorts of leadership gaps. It can help leaders transitioning into new organizations, being promoted, or preparing for leadership roles, prepping for senior leadership, leading key initiatives. It can be an integral part of building a leadership bench or for developing diverse leadership. It's in tune with leadership's present, and future.

The Platinum Rule

As the concept of coaching has evolved, so have the ideas about leadership, although those changes have been more gradual. That's why our big leap involves thinking about where leadership is going, not where it is or where it was. In short, it's time to stop relying on the leadership paradigms of the past century.

> *In short, it's time to stop relying on the leadership paradigms of the past century.*

A lot of thinking around leadership has come out of thinking about parenting. For years, companies saw themselves as "in loco parentis," hiring employees right out of school, managing their careers for them, and then taking care of them in retirement as well. So it's not surprising that past century leadership thinking had its roots in parenting. At that time, there was a push around the idea that parenting should be consistent—but since then, people have realized that consistency isn't a great ideal. What works for one of your children doesn't work for another who has a different personality or different talents and weaknesses.

The same is true in leadership. To achieve outcomes that feel fair, respectful, and productive, you can't just treat everyone the same. Workers with different backgrounds might require different approaches, distinct forms of help, development, or encouragement. To take a simple example I often use, a company might have a practice of rewarding a worker for a job well done with a public congratulations at a companywide meeting; sure, some will like being in the spotlight, but others will be mortified, and would have preferred a private note or some more personal reward.

Just being "consistent" actually doesn't work, because figuring out how to treat employees means taking differences into account.

Now think how gender, or race, might apply. Just being "consistent" actually doesn't work, because figuring out how to treat employees means taking differences into account. The workforce was much more homogenous in the past when the concept of consistency was broadly applied. Now, workforce diversity is dramatically increased, with six or more generations in the workplace, and employees have very divergent backgrounds, culture, and ways of thinking.

We all know the Golden Rule: Treat others the way you would want to be treated. Well, when you're coaching, training, managing, or leading, replace this with the Platinum Rule: Treat others the way they want to be treated. This may not be the same as how you would like to be treated.

This can be challenging, particularly for large companies. It's much easier to create a blanket set of rules and expectations, and for years that's what companies have done. But today employees expect to be treated in a more personalized manner and want their specific circumstances considered. Developing a more individual approach to employee needs is a demanding new challenge. But it's also an unavoidable one.

The underlying idea is that the majority of the population is not like you. Suppose that you are fairly similar to about 25% of the people you interact with. If you treat everyone how *you* want to be treated, you are only going to be doing the right thing for about a quarter of the people you're dealing with. Everyone else will be saying, "Why are they doing that? I don't like it."

> *The Platinum Rule: Treat others the way they want to be treated.*

My philosophy is that there are capabilities or capacities that you have to develop as a leader, but there's no single set of answers, no checklist that applies to everyone. And one reason I believe this is because it's what I did! I wasn't willing to behave like a standard corporate America male leader. I mastered the skill sets and the mindsets related to that, but I did them in my own way, and in tune with my own personality. To do that, I had to take some big leaps.

"You Can't Ask That Question"

I was born in a little town in the Blue Ridge Mountains, and when I got to school age, we moved to northern Virginia, closer to Washington, DC. I went to college at the University of Virginia, which had just gone co-ed a few years earlier. I majored in psychology, with a biology minor.

I graduated in 1981—a recession year. In Virginia at that time, if you were a woman, you had about five career options. You could be a secretary. You could be a nurse. You could be a teacher. You could be a mother. You could be a mistress to someone in Congress. That was pretty much it. I didn't want to do any of those.

But UVA had something called an externship program; you would go to a location and have the experience of working there. Mine was at Stanford University, working in the student affairs office. I loved California. So I moved to San Francisco. (That was my first big leap.)

After a few years as a social worker, which broke my heart, I ended up working at a small university as the director of residence halls, while I got a graduate degree and trained as a therapist.

During my training, I would always ask clients questions that were some variation of: *What have you done differently since the last time we got together?* And my supervisors and advisers kept telling me: *You can't ask that question.* I was told that, instead, I must go back in time, and focus on healing my subject's traumas from the past. Although healing past trauma is obviously useful to undertake, my bent was so much more toward the present and future than the past. I found this approach to therapy wasn't a fit for me. My thinking was, this wouldn't help them today!

I didn't want to delve into people's pasts endlessly, in pursuit of healing, but without really changing anything tangible in the present. I wondered, "Now what am I going to do? I just spent three years getting a therapy license!" For a few years, I switched over to teaching social psychology and similar subjects, and I started exploring training and development, and started teaching subjects like leadership skills.

I discovered they were using my question: What have you done differently since the last time we talked?

And then, around 1991, I heard about this thing called coaching. Right away, I discovered they were using my question: *What have you done differently since the last time we talked?*

As soon as I heard that question being asked, I knew that this was the approach I'd been waiting for.

Your Progress Is *Your* Job

In the early 1990s, I trained at the Coaches Training Institute, which was maybe a year old at the time, and got certified. When the International Coaching Federation was established not long after, I was among the first few hundred ICF certified coaches in the world.

I put an ad in *The Marin Independent Journal*, a paper in the county where I lived at the time, north of San Francisco. It said, "Learning to be a coach; discounted sessions." Everyone had told me it was almost impossible to get clients for this new profession, but I got about 100 responses. After spending 100 hours over a period of a couple of weeks talking with each person, I realized that most of them needed therapy as opposed to coaching, because they had to heal their past traumas before they would be able to move forward. This was surprising and a big validation for the therapeutic approach. But it wasn't the goal of coaching. Ultimately, I accepted one client.

Obviously traditional therapy has a lot of value, and coaching is no replacement for someone who needs that kind of help. And the two are not mutually exclusive. What appealed to me about coaching was that it was practical and forward looking. It was goal oriented: Here's where you are now. Here's where you want to be. How do you get there? By all means, if your past needs healing, do that work. But in the meantime, let's get your life functioning in a way that's helpful.

The one client that I took on from that initial batch of responses to my newspaper ad was the executive director of a climate change organization who wanted to influence its board and employees more successfully. That sounded interesting! And

I was able to help her. (She eventually went on to be elected to the California State Assembly.)

My practice grew, and after about a year, I realized it was becoming too burdensome for me. I was feeling too responsible for my clients' lives. Clients kept asking me what I thought they should do, instead of doing the work to uncover what they wanted. They were looking for me to direct their lives.

At the time I had about 25 clients, and I proceeded to have the same conversation with each one of them. The message I sent was essentially, "I feel like I'm doing too much work on your behalf, and you're not doing enough work on behalf of yourself."

Every one of those people laughed—and agreed.

I wasn't laughing. What I'd realized in my first year of private practice is that my clients' progress isn't my job. It's *their* job. The function of a coach is to be the sounding board for clients, the neutral observer and mirror that reflects back what they see and hear from the client. The goal is to deepen their introspection, guide them to a greater self-awareness that allows them to make hard decisions, challenge them to shift their mindsets to the next level, and to champion and encourage them when they do.

So I said, "Here are your options: You can step up and take more responsibility for your own professional life, and we can keep working together. Or you can pause until you're ready to do that. Or we'll just wrap up, because maybe you don't have the time, motivation, or agency for this right now."

Half of my clients left. But in the long run, that was the right step to take. (Another big leap.)

The ones who stayed really made progress. They took ownership of their own development instead of relying on me to "make them do it." And so did the people that came in the door next. Soon enough, I found myself coaching in corporations.

I did not set out to target the business world. In fact, I was a little bit anti-establishment. And I had to get used to being the only female on the executive floor, or sometimes in the building, who was not a secretary.

But the business world matched my skill set, and my personality. I had this very practical bent around making a change and having an impact. It's not good enough to just think about it or even to heal past trauma. That is just the first step. That healing, or new thinking, or changing mindset has to result in doing something different. I was good at helping people create actions, behaviors and results based on this internal change—and there was a real need for it in companies where impact and results are measured and desired. I ended up with a successful executive coaching practice from 1996 to 2014 starting with the Fortune 100 companies (who have all been doing exec coaching for years) and adding venture-backed and high-growth startups after 2006. After retiring from my coaching practice, I began to explore operating a business myself, eventually co-founding a coaching software company.

The Gasp

This brings us back to the big leap.

Part of a first coaching session is about starting to identify how the person is thinking. And again it's crucial for the coach to remain open to the coachee as an individual with a distinct personality and style—a green suit—who has to be treated as such. If I'm the coach and I'm a guy, and I just treat everyone like they're a guy similar to me, that might have been acceptable in 1950, but it probably shouldn't have been—and it's definitely not going to work now. Instead, it's about finding the leadership approach that works best for the coachee—who may, for starters, not be a guy. To do that, I have to understand some of their thinking. So in the first session, I ask lots of questions.

But I'll also drop a couple of pointed comments or questions to see what's underneath the surface. That can mean asking questions that might reveal what's blocking or restraining the client, or causing them to lose confidence or be less impactful than they could be. For instance, I once asked a CEO if he was actually unhappy being in that role—something he'd never been asked and that blew the conversation wide open. The idea is to push them past their standard talking points and rationale for their approach or behavior. The "bomb" cracks the facade. I call this "cracking the egg." This is part of the push for identifying a big leap right away, not spending hours talking about the past.

I once met with a first-time CEO who needed a coach and was interviewing four or five candidates. I was last, and by the time I arrived he'd picked one of the others, but I said I'd meet him anyway, since I was already there.

He told me his stories about what was going on and what he thought he needed, and I listened. And eventually I dropped a bomb. "So this is all a big power struggle," I said. "It's about free-floating power. If the CEO doesn't take up all their power, it becomes available to others to take up." I told him about a situation I'd seen in which a CEO's admin had basically been running the company. "The big leap I'd work on with you," I said, "is learning how to fully take up your power as the CEO. I don't mean power over other people, I mean the power of your role."

What you're looking for, as a coach trying to guide a coachee to their big leap, is a reaction that's almost a gasp. That's a signal that we've zeroed in on something meaningful, and the sessions that follow are going to be something more than the same old thing in the same old comfort zone. I don't remember if this

CEO literally gasped, but his reaction was visceral. "I want to work with you," he announced.

I didn't make that observation and suggestion as a gambit to win a client. I did it because that's what the big leap is all about. If I can identify what the one thing is that will move the needle for that person in the first session, then it starts the coaching off with a bang. It's not that we don't do other things down the road—the details still take time. But instead of slowly ramping up, I want them to say right away: "Oh, my God, that's the thing!" It's so motivational. They have been trying to figure it out on their own, so to suddenly have a partner who can see and name the thing they have been struggling with is profound.

The risk can be that it doesn't always feel good for someone that you just met to say, "Here's what the issue is." Sometimes people react to that, and it could be a sign that they don't want to do the work. That's okay with me because then my approach might not be the right fit for them. They might not be ready for a big leap.

They have been trying to figure it out on their own, so to suddenly have a partner who can see and name the thing they have been struggling with is profound.

Coach: Here are some ideas for how to identify the Big Leap. Which one of these attracts your attention?

1. Be open. Don't go in with preconceived ideas. Whatever it is you think at first, and whatever it is they *say* first—that's *not* it!

2. Listen for thinking or language that doesn't resonate or make sense. The big leap is never the first thing they talk about. They might mention what really matters in passing after a while, or it may be layers under the surface.

3. Look or listen for incongruence between what the person says and does, and get curious about it. (They say they want A, but are doing B. Why?)

4. You have to see into the future. See quite a few steps down the road, see where this person's movement is taking them. Take it out a number of steps until you can identify the right leap.

5. In a neutral way, name your first intuition of the "big leap" to the coachee and notice their reaction to it.

6. Ensure that what you identify is of significant scale (i.e., it can't be conceptualized as only an action). If it's not a stretch for them, it's not a leap. It has to feel like jumping off a cliff for them.

7. Get the gasp. It's not a leap if they don't feel it is much bigger than they were contemplating. If they can do it right away, it's not a leap, let alone a big leap. Big leaps require time and development. It needs to be something that makes them suck in their breath.

Coach: How do you plan to use this? With whom?

CHAPTER

2

Letting Go of Outdated Thinking

> **Coach: I gave you a few ideas last time about taking the Big Leap.**
>
> *Yeah, those were great! I'm excited!*
>
> **Coach: So what have you actually done differently, to act on those ideas?**
>
> *Ummmm . . .*

Much of the real work in a coaching engagement doesn't actually happen during the actual sessions. Those meetings are vital, of course. But the real work—the real effort to take the big leap, not just identify or imagine it—happens between sessions. And sometimes it takes a little while for that reality to sink in.

Frequently, in fact, I'll start a second session by following up on specific suggestions or thinking from the first meeting—ideas that the coachee was enthusiastic about. But have they really acted on those ideas? Done something concretely different? About 75% of the time, the answer is no.

Much of the real work in a coaching engagement doesn't actually happen during the actual sessions.

That's okay. For starters, it's human nature. Plus, taking a big leap is scary! It can also be overwhelming. Most of all, it takes a lot of letting go—letting go of assumptions that have served you well in the past, of the comfortably familiar, of ways of viewing and being in the world that you've long taken for granted.

So I hope you agreed when I made my opening argument that the time has come to get past one-size-fits-all approaches to training, management, coaching. But has your view about this really changed yet? Have you thought through (let alone acted on) what a more nuanced and effective approach to developing leaders would entail? Probably not. Again, that's okay. It takes time. It takes thinking through which of your assumptions, habits, and old beliefs have become outmoded. You have to

You have to get unattached to the way things have been up to now. And that takes some work.

get unattached to the way things have been up to now. And that takes some work.

Here's an example I've seen many times that helps make the point. Most of us start in the work world as individual contributors. You're given work to do, and you do it yourself. That's your job. But let's say you get promoted. Now you're supposed to have other people do the work, and you're supposed to manage them.

Invariably, newly promoted people can't delegate. Every new manager has multiple reasons why. "Well, I can do that better myself. And I can do it faster." "I know what I want." "I can't explain it well enough to the other person." "Time is short; they won't be able to do it but I can do it in a day."

Leaders have to learn to let go of doing everything themselves, because that's definitely not their job anymore. In fact, their job now is specifically to get other people to do tasks better than they can themselves. Even so, it's like peeling their fingers off of each of those reasons until finally, they understand: "Oh, delegation is my job. Okay, let me figure out how to do that." Unless they can let go of how they are used to thinking and operating, they won't delegate and they end up undermining themselves because not only are they trying to manage the work, but they're also trying to do all of it on their own. Later, they realize it, but in the moment, they are just blind, they cannot see it.

The same thing is true for individuals and organizations: You can't move forward without letting go of your old ways of doing things.

The same thing is true for individuals and organizations: You can't move forward without letting go of your old ways of doing things.

The Trouble with Popeye

In the early part of my coaching career, really the first 15 years or so, I only coached men—white men—because those were the majority of people in the senior leadership ranks. Of course, that changed. First I started to have a few clients who were men of color. By the early 2000s, some Fortune 500 companies had started promoting women. Around that time, I also moved over to coach a lot more venture-backed companies and smaller bio-techs, where there were more women and a lot more diversity in leadership.

To be sure, the diversity numbers are still scandalously low. Last time I checked, for example, just 53 of Fortune 500 CEOs were women, a bit over 10%.[1] But there's been enough change that we are long overdue to rethink some of the pillars of leadership theory that date back a half century or more, because the idea of who and what "a leader" can be has changed. That's even more true if you agree that the kinds of development that have been available to the C-suite ought to extend deeper into the organization. And, again, if we don't let go of old ideas, we can't move forward.

For instance, you've almost certainly heard of the Myers-Briggs Personality Indicator—a self-assessment quiz that has its takers locate themselves within four binaries, introversion/extraversion, sensing/intuition, thinking/feeling, and judging/perceiving.[2] It's been around for more than half a century. And even if your organization doesn't use it, there's a good chance that it has in place some form of assessment system that descends from Myers-Briggs. Corporations have had a love/hate relationship with this form of assessment going back to at least the 1970s and I've certainly encountered it many times.

Basically, Myers-Briggs and its spinoffs are self-reports: You assess yourself in order to determine your type. Even if it's in the form of a test, it's still a self-assessment. This has some uses, but human beings invariably don't know or understand quite a few things about themselves. It can foster an approach I call the Popeye approach: "I am what I am and that's all that I am." In other words: "I'm an ENFP"—or whatever—"so you all have to deal with an ENFP. I don't care if you like it or not, that's how it is."

This isn't really a very useful approach—for anybody.

I like a different model that came up in the same time frame, but that is more about the perception of others. Because succeeding in a company situation is often more about how others perceive you; whether they perceive you as a leader or not is probably more important than how you perceive your own personality.

The model I prefer is called Social Styles, and it's purely behavioral. It helps you observe what you see others do in an interaction: When is this person leaning forward and when are they leaning back? Do they use their hands when they're talking? Are their hands at their side? Are they making direct eye contact or intermittent eye contact? Do they have any inflection in their voice? Or more like a monotone delivery? Are they talking fast or slow? Are they walking fast or slow? It can all be seen or heard by a camera. It's based on how they are showing up to the outside, not who they are on the inside.

The model is based on these natural behaviors, and it breaks them into four quadrants, and then four subquadrants, not unlike Myers-Briggs. But ultimately it suggests a preferred style of interaction, a person's natural style. It also helps you recognize how just because this is your natural style, or your preferred style, doesn't mean it's the style you should utilize all the time. It helps you figure out what you need to change, at least in some situations, to be more successful.

It's observational, focusing on behaviors that can be seen and heard, rather than a self-report. The goal is to identify the style of others, and to learn how and when to adjust your behaviors to accommodate others' style. That's not always the right move, but sometimes it can be—and it's a major advantage.

Power Matching

Here's an example of how understanding interaction styles can be a lot more useful than just discovering and declaring your personality type.

When I coach women, I coach them to "power match" with the men. Here's what I mean. What happens often for women is that they feel underpowered, so they'll make themselves smaller, be nicer, whatever. That doesn't work. In fact, that strategy eventually makes women mad, and then they'll try to overpower whoever is causing the problem. This doesn't work either. Underpowering means the men are stepping on them. But overpowering causes women to step on men. If you can just *match* the power, now you are on more of an even playing field.

If you can just match the power, now you are on more of an even playing field.

Women have wanted the playing field to be even for a long time; it hasn't happened, and that's a process that will take more time. But women can even the playing field themselves by power matching. So I would teach them, for instance, to respond to a hostile critique by restating it very neutrally and then responding to that.

Don't be flustered or pressed down, and don't react harshly ("You idiot!" etc.) Just stay at that same level as the speaker.

By the way, while this most often comes up with women clients, power matching can benefit anyone. I remember being on a sales call with a male sales rep, who had a very analytical, deliberate style, pitch a female sales director with 25 years experience; she just ran him over. She was saying things like "stop telling me what I already know," and he became very flustered. He needed to learn to power match.

It's both a mindset shift and a behavioral shift. You have to see yourself as equal, regardless of who the other person is or what they are doing. That's the power game. You can't be the powerless one, and you also can't be the one who's trying to overpower someone else. You have to own your power and stay there.

Once you get that, then it's easy to say stuff like, "Hey, what you're saying right there—that was the same idea I suggested two minutes ago. Glad you like it. Thanks for reinforcing it." And you can do that without the other person being ticked off and fighting with you.

I had this happen myself many times during my career. This one guy kept naming every idea of mine as his own. And by about the third time he did it, I started laughing. "Hey," I said, "I love how you're liking all of my ideas today." And then the whole group started laughing—because it had become obvious that he was restating everything I said. The next time he did it, they all laughed again, and I didn't have to say anything. He got the message.

The Compliance Mentality

The deeper issue here—the thing to really examine and perhaps let go of—is the mindset that guides most assessment systems in general. I'll start by making a broad point: Most assessment and performance review systems are really focused on evaluating skills and past performance. But it's been shown time and again that past performance and skill acquisition is not a reliable predictor of potential or future success.[3]

The dominant performance assessment styles today are really built around the idea of training. That is, the kind of training that started in response to government compliance. After the Occupational Safety and Health Administration (OSHA) was founded in 1971, the practice of training was tied directly to safety measures and other standards. Slowly, the form started expanding out to other things—technical training, soft-skills training. A "compliance" mentality was applied to almost everything. Training was "required" for success.

This compliance mentality doesn't work for everything today because each environment is so individual. Now, when you just have off-the-shelf training, it's very hard for people to apply that approach to their daily work. And some things just don't benefit from that compliance style of training. We use this basic template now for sexual harassment. Does that help? I don't think so.

And yet, this attitude remains near the core of most employee assessment and performance review processes. The roots of this style actually pre-date OSHA, and arguably trace back to the World War I era. But the interesting thing is that, in the early twenty-first century, long-established forms of performance review started to go out of style. A *Harvard Business Review* (HBR) article in 2016 reported that "more than a third of U.S. companies" had moved away from traditional performance reviews that boiled down to "holding employees accountable for what they did last year, at the expense of improving performance now and in the future."[4]

This tracks with my experience. There was a phase in the early 2000s when many companies basically said, "We hate performance evaluations, and we're not doing them."

People didn't like the performance evaluation because it is mostly a binary thinking model. You did your job, or you didn't do your job. A Likert rating scale of five might be used, but basically, it's: "Did you do your job? Did you do better than we thought or worse than we thought?" That's pretty much it. Another interesting thing is that when companies didn't do performance evaluations, they were still able to make appropriate decisions about promotion and salary.

And yet, as that same "HBR" writeup acknowledged, companies that ditched traditional performance reviews in the first decade of the 2000s were, in practice, starting to reinstate them. Why? One reason is that the very simplicity many employees resent is also what makes it attractive to businesses—mostly just because that makes it easier to implement. Performance evaluations have come roaring back.

Everybody likes the easy way. But if you take your employee and management talent seriously, shouldn't you find another way of knowing how people are performing that doesn't put people into these binary decision-making models?

To me, it seems like—particularly since the pandemic—we're in a moment of uncertainty. Almost everybody has lost their mojo, their confidence level about what they should be doing. My thinking is this: Let's not fall back to what used to work. Let's move forward and create new things that work better and are a better fit for how we work now and want to work in the future.

This is why coaching, and specifically the version of coaching that I've practiced, refined, and promoted over a period of decades, is important. It's individualized, flexible, specific. No longer can you just say, "Embody these five direct traits and you'll be successful." The world is too complex for that. So now we need a much more complex way to develop leaders; we need one that blends what they need to do in their roles with sets of capacities and who they actually are as people.

Having watched this play out, I would say the main problem is a failure to let go. The perfor-

The main problem is a failure to let go.

mance review is a familiar process—maybe nobody likes it, it's shown to be a poor use of time with limited impact but everyone is comfortable with it. It's just the way things are done.

That is exactly the reason to let it go.

Why Do I Have to Stop?

As a practitioner and teacher of Tai Chi, that practice does blend into my approach to work—sometimes by reminding me what it's like to be the one who needs to figure out what to let go of, and what to embrace. Tai Chi is a long-term practice. We like to say that after 10 years, you become a beginner. So there's always something for me to learn.

Here's an example. Tai Chi has two parts. There's a solo form, but there's also an interactive form that's called pushing hands, which is like empty hand sparring. You're just using your hands against the other person's hands or body. There's no padding or anything. It's also not gender exclusive: Women and men push hands together. Which is very interesting, because in the martial arts, as in most sports, competition is often separated by gender.

Anyway, there was an early moment in my practice when I was working on pushing hands—on that interactive part—and my teacher was trying to teach me this one push, which is called a brush knee push. And I could not get it. I just couldn't do it. It involved a movement I could execute in solo form, but I could not do it in an interactive situation.

I couldn't do it for a year. And then I still couldn't do it in my second year. Then, finally, in the third year, something clicked—and I did it!

And I did it in a class where everyone was in pairs. After all that time I suddenly was like, "Oh, my God, I did that!" So I started doing it a whole bunch of times—I did it about five times with that person I was paired with. And then we changed partners—we changed every 15 minutes or so—I started doing the same thing with my new partner.

After maybe 10 minutes my teacher came over and he said, "Stop doing that push."

I couldn't believe what I was hearing.

He said, "You know how to do it now. You need to stop doing it."

And I just freaked out. I was practically yelling at him. "Are you kidding me? It took me three years to get that push and now you're telling me not to use it?"

"That's exactly what I'm telling you," he said. He's very funny; he just walked away.

I was incredulous! "I don't even get to celebrate that I finally got this push?" I said.

"Right," he said, not even looking back at me.

So I had to stop doing that push. But later I asked him: "Why did you do that? That was so brutal."

"You liked it too much," he said. "If you don't stop, you're going to use that push all the time. And you will become overly attached to it. Because you put so much into getting it, your level of attachment is equal to that effort you put in." And then he said, "You'll never be a good martial artist if you only have one push."

He let that sink in. Did I want to celebrate that one push—or did I *really want* to be a good martial artist?

"Becoming a good martial artist means you cannot keep doing that push," he continued. "You have to go on to the next push—whatever it is. You've got to let it go. No matter how much effort you put into it."

I let it go. Because now I knew what I really wanted, not just a push but a whole repertoire of pushes and responses. I wanted to be a martial artist, not a one-push wonder.

The same is true for leaders. You could be great at communication or accountability or something else. But any single skill by itself doesn't create good leadership. In fact, any strength taken too far or relied on too heavily can become a weakness. You can be a great detail person and check every task off your list, for example, but when future thinking or complex problem solving is needed, this singular focus is no longer a strength. It's a vulnerability.

Putting People in Boxes

There's a theme that unites these familiar, comfortable processes that I'm encouraging you to let go of. And that theme is a direct descendent of the attitude I encouraged you to take with a Big Leap in the first chapter: the idea that there is a single standard that every potential leader must adhere to. That idea has come to be institutionalized and formalized, not because it's right, but because it seems quantifiable and transferrable. It endures because it's familiar, and convenient.

Which brings us to the famous "nine-box talent review," first developed by McKinsey in 1970. It is still widely used 60 years later.

As the name implies, it's a 3×3 grid (in case you haven't heard of it). The details can vary but speaking broadly the two axes are "performance" and "potential." The horizontal axis tracks performance and the vertical axis represents potential. A person slotted in the top right corner has the highest potential and the highest performance. And if you go down to the bottom left corner, they have low potential and low performance. Companies use this grid to identify who they should support or who they should promote.

Now, maybe in 1970, when so much of corporate America was white and male, that worked. In reality, it probably didn't, even back then. But now, it certainly doesn't work.

For starters, much of the nine-box approach depends on assessing potential, and we now know that people can have a lot of bias around what potential looks like. Too often, it doesn't include women and members of minority groups as leaders. It's just a subjective judgment. And what I have seen happen in corporations is groups of leaders will get together and place employees in these boxes. It's a purely verbal conversation: "Oh, I think this person has potential, and I think this other person has potential—but I don't think this person has potential."

> *Much of the nine-box approach depends on assessing potential, and we now know that people can have a lot of bias around what potential looks like.*

That's where bias comes in. Because if it's just up to you or me to decide who has potential, how are we determining that through our own set of biases? It's a system that doesn't account for the nuances and potential bias around different cultures, different skin colors, and different genders. As Stephen T. Hunt, who specializes in human capital research for SAP, has bluntly put it: "9 boxes don't reflect reality."[5] Employees often don't understand how and why they've been slotted, or how to move forward, and management is left with assessments that don't reflect reality.

In fairness, practically every assessment system puts people in boxes. But the reason I like the Social Styles approach is that it can be used to help people step beyond their "box." In contrast, some of the most familiar and ingrained systems have the opposite goal or at least the opposite effect: They seem designed to categorize people, and that's it: Now you're just stuck in a box. Literally.

Change Mindsets to Change Behavior

Today we're in a totally new place in terms of talent and how companies work, and yet we are operating as if we were in a place similar to the past.

At the time these tools were developed, many people stayed at one or two companies for their entire career. Now, the average tenure for an individual worker is 4.1 years.[6] It's even less for younger workers. You cannot use the same tools you used when you expected a leader to stay for 20 years or more, when you now know they might stay for just 3.

You have impatient, younger generations who want to advance quickly. You have people who are more interested in having work that they're passionate about than the money they earn. It's a much less predictable environment. To take a recent example, think about the whole remote/hybrid scenario that the pandemic made commonplace.

In the 1970s and 1980s, maybe even into the 1990s, there was still kind of a postindustrial frame of reference. The homogenous workforce back then both resulted from and reinforced a certain kind of management, which was very top down. People at the top determined if you have potential. Now, it doesn't work that way—or it shouldn't. But now we're deep into a new era, still being sorted out, and it's just very different than the structure of the past. So why are we using ideas from a half century ago, or longer?

That's why we need to let go of familiar leadership tropes, and replace them with new, more refined, and more nuanced strategies. Let's look for new ways to develop talent that's faster, more impactful. And let's figure out how to shape not just behavior but also mindsets. Let's get past these top-down, one-size-fits-all, put-it-in-a-box systems, and pursue strategies that are more personalized and differentiated for individuals.

"Problem Children" and Other Things HR Sees

The truth is, I don't often find people in the executive function who are all that interested in a radical change in approach to cultivating leadership and talent. But along the way, I have found many people in the Human Resources function wanting to do just that.

They often have a broader view of the company in terms of employee satisfaction, and employee engagement. They see people that they know have potential being passed over. And HR knows who the "problem children" are—leaders, managers, leaders, sometimes individual contributors in the organization, who repeatedly have interpersonal problems with other folks. When these people get promoted anyway, HR sees the reaction of the people around them.

Sometimes these difficult folks are just mean and rude and demanding. But if they get the results, they may get promoted. They're not good leaders or good managers. They're getting work done by force. None of that is really being captured by traditional measures, unless HR has the ability to weigh in. In general, exec leadership may not have a window into any of this. They don't see the impact on retention or engagement or productivity. Their old mindsets keep them thinking that leading by command and control works. Recently, a number of large corporations are demanding employees come back in the office full time or be fired. This seems like a re-engaging of old thinking and certainly not in line with the current environment.

For much of my career, I have been in the training and development functions. Because of that, I got to hear from hundreds of people about how they were developing—or not—in any organization. At the same time, I often work directly with company leaders. The upshot is that I've learned the top leaders need

The effectiveness of what they've "always done" has declined over time.

help—but so do people deeper down in an organization. Of course, it's really tough to lead a company. But the next layer down often needs attention because they're the ones who have people on top pressing down, and people below pressing up. So they really need help!

Over time, I've found that at any organization where people at the top had experience with coaching, they have been supportive of extending that mentality deeper into the management ranks. And often I think what they didn't realize—like the proverbial frog in water that gradually comes to a boil—is that the effectiveness of what they've "always done" has declined over time, because the external environment has changed so dramatically. Coaching has taken off in the past 10 years because it is personalized, and customized to the individual leader. It deals with individuals, but it recognizes how context can vary, and how much that matters.

Reimagining Potential

Let's go back to the example of the new manager who needs to learn to delegate. That person is thinking, *I have a deadline on Monday, and it's gonna be a lot faster if I just do it myself. I can do it better than anyone on the team. I need to just do it and get it right.* A very practical, performance-oriented response! But ultimately a counterproductive one in the long run.

So how do you shift that thinking? You need to convince this new manager that it's okay to let go. Let go of the old way of doing things, on a personal level. And on a higher level, too.

It's not that managers and companies that stick to traditional practice are trying to do something bad. It's that—just like the new manager who keeps trying to do their prior job—they're using old thinking to try to be successful in a new environment. As a company, what I want is employees who are dedicated to the work; who do their jobs; who are skilled, conscientious, and committed. I also want employees who are growing and learning and continuously evolving because the external environment continues to change and evolve. Beyond that, I want to find ways to unleash potential in employees. The company is actually going to be more successful as a business as a result.

The trickiest part of this is recognizing potential. I've already described some of the ways that sticking to tradition can cause a company to miss potential in today's more diverse workforce. But there are more. Maybe a potential leader who happens to be more introverted has potential that might not be obviously visible, for example, or at least not visible in the ways you are measuring potential. You don't realize this until it sinks in that you're having a giant retention problem, and you're less able to promote from within. Which is an expensive problem to have.

Avoiding the Easy Way

In the arc of a coaching relationship, there are moments of uncertainty. It's clear that you're taking risks, but it's not guaranteed what the outcome will be. It takes being able to sit in that interim place a little while. It takes some time to realize, "Okay, I'm not going to be doing it that old way. But I don't know what the new way is yet."

The very tempting alternative will be to fall back to the old ways of doing things. That's true for individuals, and it's true for organizations. Even now, it's so much easier for a company to default to traditional ideas of who "looks like" a leader. It's not just in the United States, but as we've seen, we still aren't able to elect a female president. And a lot of that has to do with how people see leadership: still something in the vein of a Kennedy face.

The tools that I'm suggesting you let go of were mostly created in the framework of leadership looking like a particular kind of person. And that view drastically limits the talent that may be available to you. The key—to go back to the nine-box paradigm—is to open up how you think about potential.

The truth is, it's hard to identify potential. It's way more complicated than a bunch of off-the-shelf tests or some from-the-hip chat among managers with very similar backgrounds and trajectories. Past performance can be boiled down to activity, action, outcomes. Potential is a more perception-based idea. That makes it harder, but also makes it more exciting. Potentially.

This should be obvious, but too often it isn't obvious to top management at all that it's in their best interest to see potential in places that they're currently overlooking. Potential, that is, may not look the way they have traditionally seen it.

What that means to you will depend on your specific situation—but the implications are very real no matter what that situation may be. If you're up-and-coming and ambitious in an organization, and looking to be more visible, there's a lot of ways to get to the goal. You don't have to get to the goal by emulating an old-school paradigm and running down everybody in your way. You can zigzag. You can jump. You can go around. There are lots of ways to get to the goal.

If you're a leader, or an executive, or anybody responsible for cultivating and promoting talent, then you need to learn to adjust your lens on what a good leader looks like. Recognize that it goes beyond any five-traits model that you've been indoctrinated in. That narrow view of leadership is going to cause you to fail to recognize the potential that's right in front of you.

Either way, the first step is letting go. All these decades-old systems seem very efficient: boiling down personalities and performance to numerical data that provide an easy-seeming shortcut to actual judgment. But these systems are not efficient at all. Quite the opposite, in fact!

It's hard to admit it, but a core attraction of traditional assessment schemes is that they're codified and scalable—so much easier than doing the deeper work of truly gauging and cultivating talent and potential! So it's easy to assume that such a system must be not only the most efficient, but also the most productive.

But I'm here to tell you that this assumption is wrong. The reality is that letting go of old ideas is the true path to unlocking potential, in your leadership ranks or in yourself. Sticking with the familiar, scalable alternatives that we've all experienced is certainly easier. But it's unlikely to be the path to get what you want—what you really, really want.

> *The reality is that letting go of old ideas is the true path to unlocking potential, in your leadership ranks or in yourself.*

Coach: Here are some ways to let go of old ideas that aren't helping anymore.

1. Pay attention to what you are *putting up with* or *tolerating*. These things are usually tied to outdated beliefs.

2. Identify the situations when you are working too hard to create what you want.

3. Notice how your old thinking mindsets are limiting you or not getting you what you want.

4. Question why you are so attached to an idea or approach.

5. Get comfortable with not knowing. You might need to let go of the old before you know what the new is.

6. Switch the channel: Give yourself permission to explore new ideas and thinking.

7. Enjoy the electric charge of getting "current."

8. Believe that you can replace outmoded thinking with new approaches that are more successful in today's environment.

Coach: Which one of these would help you let go of the old most easily?

What Do You (Really) Want?

> **Coach: So did you try what we talked about last time?**
> *Actually I did. And it really did feel good to let go a bit. But . . .*
> **Coach: Yes?**
> *I'm not sure it's what I wanted.*

Here's something that can happen early in a coaching relationship: The coachee does start to let go of old habits and assumptions, and follows through with some new action, way of thinking, or approach. And . . . they're not happy about how it played out. "I tried that," they might say, "and it didn't exactly go the way I wanted it to." Or maybe it was just too scary so they tried a safer, half-measure version of the idea. Or maybe it simply felt like it didn't work, and now they're wondering if the new idea really represented the proper framework.

This, actually, is progress. It means it's time to revisit what the coachee wants—what they really want. It's a crucial question, and it should be no surprise that it can take a few tries to get the answer right.

The best coaching and training expertise in the world can't help a business that doesn't know what it really wants.

This is not just a question for the coachee. Companies looking to upgrade their leadership, improve their overall culture, and make the most of the potential in the organization now and in the future, need to go through the same process. The best coaching and training expertise in the world can't help a business that doesn't know what it really wants.

Any Road Won't Do

There's a really nice quote from *Alice in Wonderland* that I often use. Alice meets the Cheshire Cat and asks, "Which way should I go?" The Cheshire Cat asks where Alice is headed, and she answers that she doesn't know. "Well," the Cheshire Cat replies, "then any road will do."

If you don't know what you want, then all the energy and effort you can muster hardly means a thing. If you don't know what kind of leaders you want in your organization, then pretty much any old development program is fine because it doesn't matter. You're not heading anywhere. There's no goal, there's no outcome, there's nothing. You're just doing activity. The same thing is true for a coachee in a one-on-one engagement.

So you have to get to: What do you want—really, really want?

This takes hard work and effort, and I'll go into detail throughout this chapter. But I'll start with this quick sketch of an overview. One place to start is trying to pick out or name a single change or outcome you believe you want, and then examining what you've been doing that's *not* getting you to that place. This tends to be a smaller, more concrete desire, and rarely in the realm of a true "big leap." It's more like the first step.

A couple of things can happen. One is you expose disconnects. The clearer you get on what you really want, the easier it is to let go of everything that's not getting you there. You want to build an organization addressing twenty-first-century needs (a diverse workforce or leading in a volatile environment, for example) but you're relying on methods developed in the 1970s. That realization leads directly into a more focused set of goals, addressing the unpredictable ambiguity of the modern work environment and so on.

On the other hand, maybe what you learn is that what you really, *really* want isn't what you've been saying. You say you want retention; what you really want is fast development, because you are likely not going to change the fact that employees stay in their jobs for a much shorter time than in the past. You say you want agile leaders, but what you really want is leaders who follow protocol, because even though agile is a buzzword, your company culture is very structured and employees are actually not rewarded for their agility. You say you want measurable development, but what you really want is confidence that your leaders are up to the task of your business, and data doesn't necessarily equal confidence. You say you want leaders who operate in a specific framework because you think a structured approach to decision-making would be more effective, but what you really want is leaders who can make the best decision even when there isn't a lot of information.

> *On the other hand, maybe what you learn is that what you really, really want isn't what you've been saying.*

Again, it can be difficult to answer this question of what you really want, but it's one that I ask over and over. Because until you do have an answer—the right answer for you or your organization—then, as the Cheshire Cat said, any road will do. Because whichever direction you choose, at best you'll end up making the right choice by accident; at worst you'll go the opposite way altogether. Or, in many cases, you'll just keep doing what used to work but no longer does.

The Long Shadow of *in Loco Parentis*

Finding the right answer may feel particularly challenging for organizations right now.

Through my coaching career, I've seen a lot of big changes happen. Some are obvious, like the change from only coaching white, male executives to coaching a variety of people. But some changes are not so obvious, and one in particular is important to

understand: a whole shift in the
environment that's so deep, and has
been so gradual, that a lot of people
never really noticed it happening.

> *There has been a whole shift in the environment that's so deep, and has been so gradual, that a lot of people never really noticed it happening.*

One of my big clients when I was
coaching was a major company near
the top of the Fortune 500. For years
this firm hired people right out of
their schooling, whatever level that was, and often kept them
through retirement. This was built into the organization. And
then—maybe in the late 1990s, early 2000s—they decided to
rethink that approach. Partly this was just a practical decision,
but it also represented the deeper shift that I'm talking about.

When I first entered the workforce, many employers had an
attitude that the company operated *in loco parentis*—"in place of
parents." In other words, employees were essentially like children, overseen and taken care of for the entirety of their career.
Among other things, that meant that
the company basically planned your
career for you, managing your
growth, development, and even your
retirement. Companies felt like they
were in this parental role, taking care
of that employee for their lifetime.

> *Companies felt like they were in this parental role, taking care of that employee for their lifetime.*

It's an approach that was left over from the 1950s, but some
held on to it well into the 1970s, 1980s, and beyond. Of course, it's
not that way anymore. Gradually, companies started realizing that
their best employees were independent individuals who could
make their own career decisions. They also realized trying to
maintain this approach wasn't financially sustainable. (I remember some employees being shocked and dismayed at the idea of
managing their own careers.) Either way, things changed—
permanently. And as younger generations came into the workforce that didn't have that same "lifetime employment" experience

or expectation, they weren't willing to put up with companies acting like the parent.

Things started changing, and some companies started putting things in place for what these newer workers (really, really) wanted. But that hasn't always been a smooth or easy process.

Hiring Adults

Think about the rise of remote work—which started, of course, well before the pandemic. It was a way to accommodate what certain valued employees, particularly those in tech functions, really wanted. And it seemed to pay off for companies who wanted this variety of talent.

But then, many companies started to have second thoughts. They decided: "We need to make sure we're getting our money's worth out of these people." And that led to the rise of monitoring employee activity from afar—tracking which websites you're visiting and so on. Are you working? Or are you scrolling Social?

Everyone, of course, hated that. And maybe it is the more traditional companies who are trying to make sure employees are working. But it's a very clear example of how failing to let go of the old (the *in loco parentis* mode, in this case) gets in the way of a company figuring out what it really, really wants. Is the goal to track busy-ness? Or is it to have workers who truly produce? Because the irony is that when people in the pandemic started working from home, their productivity went up dramatically!

At my company we state this in our employee handbook: We hire adults, we don't hire children who need protection or supervision. Lately we have even experimented with offering Fridays off and found that there was no loss of productivity. Every week that we had a four-day week, I would say 90% to 95% of people still did five days of work, just in four days.

Sure, there's always that 5% or 10% that aren't doing what they're supposed to be doing or slacking off. But those people are going to emerge as an issue no matter what, and that can be handled in the usual ways. So are you really going to try to police the 10% in a way that alienates the 90%? Why would you go to the trouble to put all of those controls in place when most people are doing what they want (working remotely)—and, by being productive, doing what *you* want?

Mommy Benefits

That's just one example of how the ghost of the *in loco parentis* mentality can complicate the process of companies figuring out what they really want. And honestly, the same is true for many leaders, managers, and even ambitious and independent-minded employees.

The old attitude created a real sense of security. Which is why, just to be clear, I'm not judgmental about that attitude, or why it remains hard to shake. In a way, that corporate approach had all sorts of positive effects. It helped create a whole middle and upper-middle class, offering lots of folks the stability and security to, say, buy a house. There's a lot to be said for it.

But the generation that really benefited from that thinking has by now pretty much retired. And the new generations that have come along didn't have the same upbringing. They saw that stability and security weren't necessarily going to remain available, to them at least, so they want something different.

But the ghost of *in loco parentis* still hasn't disappeared entirely. This youngest generation that's coming into the workforce right now—often, many of their parents did everything for them. They may not imagine sticking with one company for an entire career, but many actually want whoever their employer is to do everything for them as well. They like the idea of a company that will do "everything" for them from feeding them to doing their laundry.

Think of these as "mommy benefits." We're not going to offer lifelong career security—but we'll do your laundry, cut your hair, make food available so you don't have to cook for yourself. We'll take care of you And some workers want that.

Or at least, a lot of companies (especially tech startups) believe they do. But again, it's worth digging a little deeper to understand what these workers *really* want—even if they don't understand it yet themselves.

Make It Meaningful

I suspect that the companies that dole out mommy benefits are missing something—namely, that these benefits aren't truly meaningful in the long run. What's meaningful is colleagues that you trust and want to work with, work that is challenging for you, opportunity that doesn't feel too constrained, the chance to have an impact or advance a passion. Those are the meaningful things people eventually want. At some point these workers realize: "I can get free meals and a lot of money at lots of companies. But is my work meaningful?"

A recent MetLife survey of 2,600 workers found that "emerging benefits" such as paid sabbaticals and phased retirement programs—which speak to long-term commitment—were more popular and in demand than "on-site services" like free meals and dry cleaning.[1] Meanwhile, management software and metrics company Qualtrics found that the primary reasons people leave jobs were factors like "not feeling valued" and "misalignment with an organization's values."[2]

That squares with what we've seen happen at those companies that focused on providing all those mommy-benefit services:

They only worked with the youngest employees, and did little to promote long-term retention. Often those folks only stuck around until they started families.

Early in my coaching career, around the mid 1990s, I coached some folks at an upcoming tech company. The average age of a manager there at the time was 28. To have so many young managers was kind of unheard of, but I was able to see how that happened. If you were unmarried, you would be there all the time; people literally slept in their offices. And if you worked like that it was possible to advance really quickly. Once you had a family, however, you couldn't keep working and living like that, so you left.

If you're only focused on the part of your workforce that's between ages 20 and 30, that will work, more or less. But ultimately you're systematically eliminating a huge chunk of talent.

Figuring out the aftermath of in loco parentis *is a timeless challenge, but also a very timely one.*

This is why figuring out the aftermath of *in loco parentis* is a timeless challenge but also a very timely one. Plenty of companies, from established behemoths to fast-growth start-ups, have embraced new approaches, techniques, and experiments. Yet somehow, old ways keep returning, as if we can't quite go all the way with our efforts to reinvent work culture. However, I think that, no matter how much backsliding slows us down, the changes are inevitable. The thinking around the twenty-first-century work environment is so different than the last century, and I believe the newer thinking is what we really want.

Eye-of-the-Storm Wants

With clients, I sometimes have to repeat variations on the question "What do you want?" so often that I start joking about it. But it's necessary because people will come in with the goals or ideas about what they want that aren't really what they want at all.

It's what someone *told* them they should want. It's what they *think* they should do. It's an externally motivated "want." That's not a deep internal desire.

I hear constantly "This is what I want, because it worked at my last employer." And I respond: "Okay, but what do you want *now*, in this job, at this time, with this employer?" It's not the same thing.

Often, people do not fully understand what they want until they take an action that someone else suggested (or required) and realize the outcome is different than what they imagined, and doesn't match with what they wanted. Sometimes they even get the blame for a subpar outcome. Through that experience, they start to understand that identifying what they want, the big impact they can have, is critical to establish before taking action. I ask questions to help people gain clarity, until they begin to ask these questions themselves. "What are you hoping will happen if you do this?" "What would be the best possible result?" "What are you trying to avoid?" And, as many times as I need to ask, "Is this what you *really* want?"

What coaching does is try to help them get to their internally motivated desires. This process is what allows a coach to guide them more appropriately. I think of it as finding, and being, the eye of the storm. If you're just trying to do what everybody outside of you wants, you're going to end up getting pushed and pulled all over the place, "blown by the wind." Instead, you need to develop this strong inner core about what you want, your own internal compass. That way what everyone else is doing doesn't pull at you so much.

That's why I have to keep asking what clients really want. Sure, we'd have a conversation about this at the start, but then we'd have to revisit it over and over again. We have to explore what they say they're not willing to do. Does that conflict with what they say they wanted? Does that mean it's not really what they wanted after all? Or does getting what they want mean they have to do things they don't want to do? Do they want something, but not enough? Or are they ready to stand in the middle of the storm for it? When we get here—

This is what they really, *really* want.

Thinking Partners

The essence of the coaching process is getting the coachee to shift their thinking, that is, not just letting go of old ideas, but embracing new ones that will help them be more successful. As the coach, you can't just *tell* them what to do. You have to help them arrive at what they need to do. Sometimes we call this being a thinking partner.

What the coach wants to do is change the coachee's way of thinking, their belief system, mindset, perspectives. Or rather, we want to help them find their way to making those changes themselves.

Once a new perspective is embraced, then we can say, "Oh, if you're thinking about it like that, what would be the action you would take?" The coachee ends up taking a new action that's now in alignment with the new thinking. This is often very successful, and because there is no cognitive dissonance between mindset and action, the new behavior and thinking stick naturally.

But the change in thinking *must* come first. If you don't change the thinking, and you just try to make rote behavior change by practice, under stress, that supposed "change"

You have to help them find the new thinking that they really want. You have to be partners.

inevitably drops away. It's like going on a crash diet or impulsively downloading an exercise app—if it's not truly self-initiated, if it's just done as a short-term reaction to something external, it won't stick. It falls away.

So you certainly can't tell the coachee what to do. But you also can't tell them what to think. You have to help them find the new thinking that they really want. You have to be partners.

Is Being Right Really All You Want?

You might assume clients and coachees would love the idea of being thinking partners, but it's not unusual for them to resist, especially at first. Often people *want* to be told what to think, want to be told what they should want. "I'm writing you a check," is the attitude. "Aren't you supposed to make everything better for me?"

This, actually, is an offshoot of the kind of single-paradigm, one-size-fits-all, master-these-five traits approach I discussed in Chapter 1. People have been pushed to believe there is only one path, and they don't want to take a "wrong" step. So we have to convince them that there are always a lot of ways to handle any given situation or career decision, and the key to ambiguous environments is accepting that there are lots of choices, not just one choice. (I'll have much more to say about embracing ambiguity in the next section.) If all you're doing is trying not to be wrong, it takes away all the possibilities of experimenting and developing. And also the possibility of you getting what you really, really want.

Before my years as an executive coach and co-founding my current company, I was part of a training firm. We taught leadership skills and all kinds of interpersonal skills. And we used to say that being right gets the booby prize. (You can tell this was a while ago because hardly anyone uses that term anymore!) Because just being right doesn't necessarily get you what you want. In fact, it might throw you off course.

> *Just being right doesn't necessarily get you what you want.*

Let's say one of your subordinates misses a deadline. Slamming them for missing the deadline—while you are 100% right that that is what happened—isn't necessarily good leadership. It also doesn't necessarily get you what you want.

What do you want if someone misses the deadline? You want them to complete the work ASAP! So telling them they're bad, and getting mad and yelling at them and docking their pay and putting it on their performance evaluation—none of that actually gets the work done. It just creates a big distress between you and them, which could easily delay the work even more. So you could go a totally different way. And when someone doesn't make their deadline, you might say: "Hey, what's blocking you on this? What needs to happen so that this can be completed?"

You end up actually coaching your employee to complete the task, instead of just reacting out of what you think is leadership—which is telling people they have a deadline, and then telling them that they're bad when they don't meet it. That's supposedly the "right" thing to do. But it doesn't accomplish what you want.

This is why coaching always comes back to the point of getting what you want. Do you just want to be right? Is that your ultimate goal? Or do you want the work to be done? Do you want the work done in a high-quality way? Do you want your employee to actually stay, and improve, so you don't have to hire a new one? In that case, focus on what's going to help them get the work done, and stay, because doing the supposedly "right" thing is going to have the exact opposite effect.

Following the Rules Is Not Enough

The truth is, there's a big hunger out there for being told exactly what to do. That's why definitive-sounding lists are so popular: 10 Steps to Achieve X, for example, or online videos telling how to style your clothes, or do your makeup, or lose weight, or attract a partner.

But when it comes to leadership, being told how to act and what to do can only take you so far. Doing the "right" thing—meaning the expected thing, just a combination of being strict and doing what you're told and focusing on proving your own rule-following ability—can work for an early-stage manager. But even by the time you get to middle management, the strategy starts to fall apart. Now you have the people below you who want things from you, people on the side who are competing with you, and people on top are telling you what to do—sometimes contradicting each other.

I understand why people want a checklist. But I also understand that there is no checklist.

You have to develop your own way of sorting that internally through who you are, your own internal compass. It's the eye of the storm idea: Without it, you're just blown all around.

The thing is, I have met lots of CEOs and coached quite a few. And I can tell you that the idea that there's one way to be a successful leader—to execute a strategy, to run a business—is just wrong. I could not say that any of these CEOs were the same as others. They took different paths, made different decisions, adopted different styles, even within the same industry, selling the same product or services. I understand why people want a checklist. But I also understand that there is no checklist.

How to Get Beyond "Being Right"

When I was working for that training company, we would sometimes videotape executives as part of the process of trying to help them become better leaders. We frequently encountered managers who had deeply bought into a very command-and-control kind of approach because it seemed right. A lot of our work involved getting them to think beyond that. There was one senior leader at an insurance company who I still particularly remember.

Before we got involved, he had already gone through a training course, and he had received one-on-one feedback, analyzing a video of him and so on. But when the company brought us in, HR told us, "This guy went through all this training, and he's still being really authoritarian and yelling and he hasn't changed." Basically, he was a jerk to his subordinates, and it was a real problem.

So the company wanted us to send someone in to work with him individually and try to help him. My company tried with a couple of other people, and then finally turned to me and said, "You're the coaching expert, you try." (Coaching was still much less established and understood back then, so maybe it seemed exotic.)

I had already seen this guy in action, because I had been the trainer for a session with a class of leaders that he was a part of. I knew the basics and I'd seen the videos. So I went into his office for our first appointment, and he was standing there. And I said, sharply: "Sit down and shut up."

He looked totally shocked. But he was still standing.

"I said, *sit down*."

He sat down.

"What," I demanded, "is wrong with you?" I'm pretty sure I added some colorful language. I went on for a while in that vein.

But not *too* long. Because right away, he became a puddle—literally tearing up. And this is the big macho guy! His whole persona was alpha dog, but now he was on the defensive, rattled. And he said: "Why are you talking to me like this?"

"This is how you are talking to your employees," I said, lightening up just a little. "And I wanted you to understand what it feels like from their side."

He denied any such thing, of course—but I had the video. I played the clips of him that made plain the style he'd been using to browbeat his subordinates. Finally, his defenses came down. "Oh, my God," he said. "But I was just trying to get them to get the work done!"

"I know," I said. (My tone had become friendlier by this point.) "But your approach to trying to get work done *isn't working*. People are just getting upset. They're quitting. They're complaining about you to HR. And you're still not getting the work done."

I didn't even need to say the biggest point: *And you're killing your own career in the process*. I mean, it used to be accepted that bosses would yell and critique like an angry parent—and maybe that had been exactly the culture he'd experienced earlier in his own career—but even at the time this was happening, it was clear those days were ending. Yelling was not okay. So as a starting point, that was something he needed to let go of.

We talked a little of what he could do differently. He seemed to get the message, and I only saw him that one time. A month later, HR called up my company with an update: "What did you do to this guy? He's transformed."

I think mostly he just didn't understand the impact he was having. He was doing what he thought he was *supposed* to be doing to get the work done from his own experience. And he didn't understand that he was hurting everyone's feelings, and that was de-motivating them.

But one level deeper than that, I think he finally realized that he was not taking an approach that would get him to where he really wanted to go. He thought he wanted to be feared or intimidating or whatever. But that's not what he wanted. He *really* wanted to be effective, and respected. So he behaved just like the authoritarian bosses he'd dealt with coming up. And the approach he was taking wasn't doing that for him. All that stuff he was yelling might have been right, yet it wasn't getting him what he wanted.

So he decided he didn't want to "be right." He wanted to be effective, and move forward—earning the respect of his subordinates, not their fealty. And that's exactly what he did.

Next!

By now you may have noticed a pattern. Early sessions in a coaching engagement are about identifying a big leap, but then taking a step back.

It takes some work to figure out what you really want as opposed to what you think you're supposed to want. Some of that work happens in coaching sessions, but much happens between sessions. It's a process: identifying, step by step, the individual insights about your own true goals and motivations.

But then what happens? In a word: actions.

Figuring out what you want is crucial, but obviously it doesn't mean much if you don't start taking concrete steps and making real changes to achieve it, because chances are good that what you have been doing isn't creating the future that you really want.

> *It's a process: identifying, step by step, the individual insights about your own true goals and motivations.*

But you have to go through these early steps to make sure you're making moves in the direction you really want. First you figure out the big leap you need to take. Next you get rid of all these things that are stopping you from getting what you want. Finally, you reexamine and challenge what you really, really want.

Now, you're ready to really take the big leap.

Let me shove you off the cliff.

Coach: Here are some thoughts on how to figure out what you really want.

1. Unless you've done this work before, what you want is probably not what you think it is, so beware of the first things that come to mind.

2. If you are unsure what you want, start with what you *don't* want to narrow it down.

3. Look beyond one specific outcome to the *why* of your actions. *Why do I want this outcome? What do I gain by getting it? What do I lose by getting it?*

4. Consider what is in alignment with your or your company's values.

5. Overcome your fear by asking yourself "What would I want if I wasn't afraid?" "What would I want if I didn't have anything to prove?" "What would I want if I knew I couldn't fail?" "What would I want if I didn't have to please anyone else?" "What would I want if I knew I was good enough?"

6. What would you want if there are no limits? Imagine something 10 times greater than what you say you want.

7. Imagine how you will feel when you get what you really want. Is that how you want to feel?

Coach: Which of these do you want to try? Or something else?

PART

Challenge

CHAPTER

4

Jumping off the Cliff

> *I think I've made a lot of progress.*
>
> **Coach: You have.**
>
> *I've let go of old thinking, and I think I know what I really want.*
>
> **Coach: Great.**
>
> *So . . . maybe I'm kinda done?*
>
> **Coach: Oh, I'd say you're just about ready to start!**

The fourth session of a coaching engagement is often an inflection point. If the process doesn't deepen at this stage, the coachee's effort tends to fall off. They've talked about their goals and reexamined a lot of their usual thinking and old patterns. Often, they have even made real changes in the way they think about their work and their goals. And that's an accomplishment.

But it's not nearly enough to add up to a big leap. And that's why the fourth session frequently kicks off a new phase that's all about taking action: You've revamped the way you think; now it's time to act on those new thoughts and insights.

You've revamped the way you think; now it's time to act on those new thoughts and insights.

As we'll explore in the chapters ahead, this can be a bumpy process. You might try something new, based on your new thinking, that doesn't work. You may experience false starts, even failure. That's actually okay. As we'll see, a short-term failure can be a lesson in what's really obstructing your progress, but the mere possibility of facing down setbacks can be off-putting, or flat-out frightening.

After years of coaching and training and thinking about leadership, I've found that the real stumbling block at this stage isn't exactly fear of failure per se. It's the uncertainty, the risk, the impossibility of knowing what a change could mean, or how a genuinely novel action will play out. What we really need to get comfortable with, to keep moving ahead, is the unknown.

> *What we really need to get comfortable with, to keep moving ahead, is the unknown.*

The Lesson of the Lavender Suit

The truth is that when you abandon the old and embrace the new, it makes ambiguity inevitable. By definition, it means heading into a period of uncertainty about how to get what you really, really want. So you have to be willing to tolerate some ambiguity—or, better yet, embrace and make the most of it.

And it's important to make the point that this goes for companies, too. Companies need to think about what kind of leadership they're trying to cultivate. If they don't, then they run the risk that what they're doing isn't creating what they want. If a business is too rigid and cautious in its approach to leader development—if, in other words, it can't accommodate some ambiguity—it's going to miss opportunities, lose talent, and struggle to keep up with the competition. That's particularly true now, as the employee-employer relationship is rapidly evolving and changing.

But it's always been true. It was true, in fact, when I was graduating from college. In those days, the university career center would arrange interviews with potential employers. One that I signed up for was with one of the Big Eight accounting firms. (This was in 1981; we're down to the Big(ger) Four now.) I was a psych major, so I assumed if they wanted to meet someone like me it must be a people-oriented job.

So I went to the career center, and to the designated room. There was big table, and there were seven or eight men around it—all men. I said hello and introduced myself and nobody said anything. They just stared at me. I waited for a minute, thinking, "What the heck is this? Is it a joke?"

And then I just *made* it a joke. I said to myself: "Hi, Lori! Would you like a seat?" I answered myself, out loud: "Sure. Thank you very much." And I sat down in one of the free chairs. They still didn't say anything. So I continued: "Well, Lori, maybe you'd like to tell us a little more about yourself." And I basically proceeded to interview myself: I told them about my background, and I told them about my education, and I told them about what I wanted to do. I just went on a monologue for 20 minutes, because these guys didn't say anything. Even when I paused! Nothing!

Finally I said: "Okay, what questions do you have for me?" Of course, they didn't say anything. So I asked myself a couple more questions, and I answered them, and then I wrapped it up: "Great, thank you so much for your time!" I told each of them, individually, that it was nice to meet them. By then I was laughing my head off inside. What the heck was that? That was ridiculous! But I didn't think anything of it, because I was 21. What did I know?

Well, a week later, they offered me a job. I couldn't believe it. I talked to them again and they said: "Oh, you were the only one who was creative. You were the only one who was assertive, and took control of the situation. You weren't stunned into silence, you were innovative." And so on.

Fantastic. I'll take the job!

Now fast-forward to my first day at work. Right away I was told that there was a dress code: I would need to wear a black or blue suit, a certain length skirt, and a white blouse with a bow— practically a uniform. Again, I kind of laughed. Still, the next day I did wear a blue suit, because I happened to have one. But I had just graduated college, I had only three suits, and one of them was lavender, so on my third day at work that's what I wore.

I wasn't there 15 minutes before I get called to HR.

I was told: "You're not wearing the right clothing," and to go home and change. Now, this suit was completely professional; it was a designer suit, everything was the right length, I had the white blouse and bow. I said, "Whoa, if I go home and change I'd have to put on the same thing I was wearing yesterday." They were fine with that. I said, "Wait a minute, you hired me because I was innovative, creative, assertive." And they basically said, "Well, you can be all those things. But you have to wear this outfit."

I could see this was not going to work. They couldn't believe I was refusing to go home to change. "We can't retain you as an employee if you don't do that," they told me—and I guess I didn't want to be retained as an employee! So we parted ways. It all lasted three days.

In fairness, this happened in 1981—a different world from now. My company works with the descendent version of this firm now, and these days the women there are certainly free to wear brightly colored suits and tennis shoes. Times have changed a lot since then, but the experience stuck with me as an example of management saying they wanted something, but then the way the company operated was squashing exactly what they said they wanted.

This is what I learned: Here's a company that claims to want innovative, creative, assertive employees, but then it insists that they behave in specific, rule-restricted ways. This company can't deal with the reality of the unknown.

Thinking versus Doing

This is precisely the reason that coaching session four is an inflection point—it's often the moment when the rubber meets the road. Up to now we've been talking about the big leap. We've been questioning ideas that are no longer useful. We've been thinking hard about what we really, really want.

But now we've reached the place where it's time to let go of that process of self-examination and truly do something different, try something new. This is where you're not just talking about it and thinking about it—but actually *doing it*.

When people get to this point, they're very excited about the idea *of change. But then they hesitate to actually take the actions that add up to change.*

Even if they know they are stuck and they need to shift course, truly doing so feels like risking everything.

The challenge is that when people get to this point, they're very excited about the *idea* of change. But then they hesitate to actually take the actions that add up to change.

It's understandable. Often, people who are in a position to experience coaching or specialized training have enjoyed some success, or they're seen as having potential. Now they're being asked—told!—to shift course. Even if they know they are stuck and they need to shift course, truly doing so feels like risking everything.

Maybe they're going to fail. Maybe they'll look like idiots. Maybe it will be fine but still not really result in what they wanted. Maybe it involves trying something they're not good at. Maybe they don't have the skill set to do something in a new way. Maybe they're not even sure what the new way is.

There are a whole lot of reasons things can stall out right here.

All of this is pretty obvious to a coach—but, importantly, it's *not* obvious to the coachee. That's the trickiest part. The coachee is, by now, comfortable talking and thinking in new ways. And that's what they want to keep doing! It's a curious form of denial: They're all in on the *idea* of change, but to actually make that change happen is daunting.

They're all in on the idea *of change, but to actually make that change happen is daunting.*

Three Ways Forward

There are a couple of important points to make about this moment, but the most urgent issue is *How do you get moving?*

Of course, there's no one-size-fits all answer. But there are three broad strategies, which can and should be tweaked to fit the individual situation, that I've used to get people moving forward past this barrier.

Option 1: Identify, and act on, the *easiest* possible change. It can be small scale, but it's real and tangible.

Option 2: Identify, and act on, the *most impactful* possible change. In other words, maybe this is an action that will take more time and effort (like acquiring a new skill set), but it will have the most tangible impact.

Option 3: Identify, and act on, the *most enticing* change. This is just what it sounds like—the new thing they most clearly want to do.

Finding the right answer usually depends on a direct conversation. In fact, this is a moment that at my company we think of as a blunt *challenge* to the coachee. It starts in a straightforward way. Maybe: "What is the new action you are going to take?"

They'll generally come up with some sort of answer, but often they'll leave the specifics vague. So then you have to force their hand. "Okay then, how about you do that as soon as we hang up the phone?" Now they hem and haw: They can't do it today, so many meetings, etc. "Okay, how about tomorrow? How about by Tuesday?"

Eventually they'll say yes to a hard deadline. But the challenge isn't over—they might be agreeing just to end the conversation, and the next session will be a litany of excuses. Then, the coach has to press a little further: "Okay, great. And just as a gut check, what would you say is your level of commitment to taking that action, on a scale of zero to 100%?"

Often they'll just admit: "Well, it's maybe 50%. I'm kind of just agreeing because you're making me do it." At this point, you can shift and reframe the discussion: "Okay, well what would get your commitment up to 70%?"

At this stage what matters most is the shift from thinking to doing.

Now the rubber is meeting the road: You're having a real discussion, about what action they are actually willing to take. Now, tweak things until they agree to 70% commitment—then force their hand again. What can we do to get that higher? Keep refining until they get to a convincing 90% commitment. Maybe getting to that point involves scaling back the action, but that's okay. Because at this stage what matters most is the shift from *thinking* to *doing*.

Breaking through the Excuses Barrier

It's hard to overstate how important it is to start taking action, even a small action. Often the holdup is mostly psychological, so that first simple action can snowball.

Let's say an HR leader wants to initiate a new way to have performance conversations at work—maybe one that doesn't evaluate performance but evaluates alignment between the managers and their direct reports. They have it clearly pictured in their minds, and they've thought through all the stuff they want to do and why they want to do it. They have a big dream of creating this new entity that becomes a major initiative that makes a lot of impact. They can envision and describe all of it.

However, they haven't actually done anything, not even the most basic step, to get this dream under way. It's a scenario I've seen many times, and that's why I put such an emphasis on taking that first action.

It can be effective to simply be direct, and very concrete. In this case, I might say, "I want you to make a slide deck for your idea, and pitch it to three leaders in the organization who could champion your initiative." Concrete.

Inevitably, there's pushback. "Oh, I can't make a deck. I need a designer, or I can't talk to those leaders, I don't think they will like it, blah, blah, blah." No, I would assure them, you can do it. Just make a simple five-slide deck to share the idea, the thinking behind it and its potential impact for the organization . . . The goal is just to push them to the point where they say: "Yes, I'll do that." It's about breaking through that barrier—the excuses barrier.

What invariably happens once I get them to do the first step? They keep going, beyond what they promised! "Once I did those first five slides, I ended up making a pretty detailed deck. Every time I shared it, I improved it. I ended up showing it to a half-dozen people, and it's really getting momentum." Now I can stop pressing them, and start praising them—to keep the momentum going.

Collecting Nos

Here's a real example of how this can work, when tangible actions line up with authentic goals. It involved a new account executive in sales who was really having a hard time dealing with hearing "no." He knew that this was getting in the way of taking his career where he wanted it to go. It was a barrier.

So I told him: "You have to get 20 nos this week." In other words: You have to call enough people that 20 will give you a flat-out no, not even an "I'll think about it." And every time that happens, and you hear "no," it's actually good. Because that's your goal, to collect nos.

At first, he balked—he just couldn't fathom courting that much rejection. But we worked out a schedule that broke it down to a certain number of calls a day, and he promised to text me when he hit his daily "no" quota.

Well once he got going, he *kept* going. He'd make his daily quota, text me, and keep making calls. Once he got into the swing he would make about 100 calls to get his 20 nos. More to the point, in addition to the maybes, he got 10 yeses. That represented real progress toward his true goals. But he could only get there by finding a tangible action that aligned with those goals—and really doing it.

There's something about this process that's almost like physics: An entity at rest tends to stay at rest, one in motion tends to remain in motion. At its best, coaching is like a force exerted on an entity at rest. It pushes things forward a little bit. And once the change starts, once things start rolling, it builds on that momentum.

Importantly, again, there's no specific, preset form for the force being exerted that works for everybody. Collecting nos was a great idea for this sales executive, but it might be a nonstarter for someone else. What matters is finding an action that gets the motion started. The specifics will vary by individual, and that's fine: The momentum just needs to be in the direction that lines up with what they really want. I'll say more about how to keep that momentum going in the chapters ahead.

Sometimes even a small, easy-sounding change of behavior can have a major impact.

For now, I just want to underscore that the step to taking action is pivotal. Sometimes even a small, easy-sounding change of behavior can have a major impact.

Paying the Piper

One example of small change with a big impact involved a particular client of mine. He was a very seasoned executive, with potential to thrive even more than he already was. But he was also an absolute master of claiming he just *couldn't* do the things he wanted to do. "I'll have to pay the piper," he would say. Presumably he meant there would be consequences or repercussions—but he never spelled any of that out. He just kept saying: "I'll have to pay the piper." And literally anything I suggested he'd shut down the same way. He couldn't do it, because he'd have to . . . pay the piper.

I kept hearing him say this until finally I said, "Look, you keep saying this phrase over and over. And it's stopping you from going forward. So you cannot say that phrase for the next week."

At first he looked totally shocked. He didn't seem to realize how often he was saying this phrase so he was confused. And then he took it in stride, and didn't seem to think it was a big deal. "Sure," he said. "No problem."

I saw him again a week later.

"So what happened?" I asked. "Did you stop saying that phrase?

"Oh, my God—I couldn't stop myself from saying it!" he said. "I wanted to stop, but I kept saying it, all the time! In the first two days, I said it at least 25 times. It was *torture* to not say it!"

This seemingly minor challenge ended up making it really visible to him how stuck he was. We talked about it. Where did that phrase come from? Well, his dad had said it. So it was operating in some mode that came to him from his father, and that was now blocking him from doing what he wanted to do in his own life.

And even in that session, he tried to say it a couple times. "Stop," I said. "You can't say that phrase." I insisted he spend another week banishing those words from his repertoire.

The next week he came back and said, "Okay, I didn't say that phrase for the last three days."

I said that was great, and asked what he thought the impact had been. "Before I stopped saying it," he said, "it was like I just couldn't think about the future."

There's the breakthrough. In using that phrase, he was naming his fears and giving them power. In the process he was, by default, overfocusing on what any given action might *cost* him monetarily, emotionally, or how it could go bad. He was using that phrase to talk himself out of taking action, all without realizing it.

When he stopped saying that phrase, it made him realize what was going on. In those sessions, I could almost see his mind saying it—like he was trying to say it, and knew he couldn't let the words come out of his mouth. So there would be a pause: "Oh, if I'm not saying that, what should I be saying? Or what *could* I be saying?"

By the next session, he was taking steps toward the things that he had said he wanted to do. This one small action—while perhaps harder than he realized it would be—had allowed him to see the future again.

"Tell Me to Get Going"

Maybe it's just a natural human reluctance to embrace certain kinds of change, but there's a near universality to pushing back against taking even straightforward steps like the ones I've described. The tricky part is figuring out what makes any one person get moving. This is another variety of ambiguity: There's no single right formula for sparking action. It takes attention and effort, a range of different strategies that sometimes feel like trial-and-error.

The reason there's no one-size-fits-all strategy for action is that people have many different forms of resistance. I'll dig deeper into this point in the next chapter, but this stage in the process is partly about beginning to confront resistance. Some people have very intellectual resistance. Others will have rationalizations about what they "just can't do." Sometimes resistance is about fear—a fear of failure, a fear of being judged, a fear of "looking bad." Some people resist with something almost like a fog: a blank look that says, "I want to do that, but I just don't know how."

The point I want to underscore is that at this stage it almost doesn't matter why someone is resisting—there is time to delve into that later—as much as it matters punching a hole in that resistance. That's why it helps to lay down a challenge: Whatever gets them out of the fog is good, because even an action that doesn't pay off immediately will cause change. They'll come back next time and say, "Well, I did that and it didn't work. But, you know, now I know what I need to do next."

There's a really funny animated short that I saw years ago at a film festival. It was made in 1972 and it's called *Getting Started*. A sweet-looking pianist with a big round nose and a mustard-colored bowtie starts to sit down at the piano to practice—then decides to gargle first. Then he takes a phone call. Adjusts his bench. Finally he plunks a few keys, only to stop when something sounds off. (There's a mouse in the piano.) Then he takes a break, and starts talking to the mouse. "Tell me to get going," he implores the creature. "Say something, like, 'Get going.' Something like that, you know?" He talks to himself, gets distracted by the clock, straightens a picture, goofs off, paces, checks what's on TV, and daydreams about giving a command performance. Every once in a while he manages a short burst on the piano, but there's always something else to focus on instead. Ultimately he decides to accept a party invitation he'd earlier rejected. "I've got lots of free time", he says.

Getting Started captures a feeling we all know. And maybe the truest note in it is the moment the character wishes someone would tell him to "get going." Everybody needs that push some-times, however simple it sounds.

One of the most famous solutions to this challenge is "morn-ing pages"—a creative writing exercise endorsed and popularized by Julie Cameron in her famous book *The Artist's Way*. Basically it involves three pages of stream-of-conscious writing, first thing in the morning, about anything, executed quickly. "Do not over-think Morning Pages," Cameron writes. "Just put three pages of anything on the page . . . and then do three more pages tomor-row."[1] In short, this is a way for Cameron to tell you: Get going!

What I am suggesting is something comparable to saying, "Okay, by tomorrow, you have to get two paragraphs on the page. I don't care if it's good or bad. I don't care what it's about, but by this specific time—maybe as soon as you hang up the phone—write those paragraphs. Just write something. The idea is it starts to get this flow going. Do something that takes a step in the direction where you're headed. Start that forward motion.

Wait, Are We Just Starting?

Some of you might be wondering why I'm saying so much about "starting," this deep into the process. This can come up with coachees. *Wait a minute*, they might say, *I thought I started weeks ago!* They've already been on a journey to figure out what they want and what to let go of, so they feel like they've been doing their equivalent of morning pages for a while.

Fair enough. The difference is that by the time you get to the stage of starting to take actions, you need to have all that prelimi-nary thinking work behind you—so that when you *start* to take actions, they're leading you where you want to go. Maybe it helps to think of this inflection point not as starting, but as starting 2.0.

To stick with the morning-pages comparison, maybe you spent a few weeks doing your pages, but they were really just a stream of consciousness. And ideally you learned something from that. Maybe you learned you want to focus on some particular subject—let's say it's cats, just to make things easy. So now your pages need to be about cats. What about them? At this stage, that might not matter. But it has to be about cats. Further refinement will follow, but for now, this increased focus is progress.

In short, this is a moment for a coachee to start to narrow down toward the direction in which they want to go. It's time to stop musing about anything and everything. It's time to focus, so in that way, they're just getting started.

Just Make It to the Deck

Another idea from the martial arts applies really well here. Tai Chi requires daily practice. And it's very difficult for people to get a daily practice going consistently. So we have a concept called Maximum and Minimum Practice. The idea is, if you think you have to practice, say, an hour, every day, it's going to be very hard to get started after a very short time. You'll think, "I just don't have an hour today, so I'll skip it, but I'll make sure to do an hour tomorrow." And tomorrow something else will come up to keep you from practicing. And then your barely started habit begins to fall off.

So instead of that, we say: "If you don't have time for your *maximum* practice, then have your *minimum* practice instead. Maybe that's only a few minutes. I have days when all I can do is get to my practice space—outside, on the deck—and put in my minimum, two-minute meditation. Even that small act breaks through the resistance.

Because the hardest part is just to get out to the deck. There are *so many* reasons not to. The dishes are there, the cat's doing something, somebody needs my help, I hear my email and slack pinging, whatever. But you have to work to get past that resistance. Once I'm there, in my space, and I do my scanning meditation for two minutes, I often end up thinking: "Oh, this is good. Let me stay here a little longer. Oh, well, let me just do this little thing. Oh, let me practice this." And I end up practicing much more than the minimum.

Once you start taking action, you'll want to take more action. It becomes self-generating.

It's that minimum activity that gets you through the wall of resistance. Once you start taking action, you'll want to take more action. It becomes self-generating.

The challenge in the context of reshaping a career or building leadership skill is that the path may not be as clearly structured as Tai Chi. It takes a lot of work to make sure you're pointed in the right direction. That's why there's so much thought and consideration building up to those first breakthrough actions.

If I want to go north, step by step, then that first step that gets you moving needs to be a north facing step. My Tai Chi practice doesn't just require me to get out of the house; it requires me to get to the deck. If I go out the front door instead, I do something completely different—I get in the car, I leave my practice behind. Wrong direction.

You need to move in the direction that's going to get you what you really, really want. But paradoxically, that's exactly why the resistance shows up: Because by this point in the process you've put in the time to figure out what you really want, and the part of you that's afraid that you're not gonna get it throws up all this resistance. Many people—maybe most—would rather *not try* and not get what they want, than *try and fail* in getting what they want. Actually, that's why a coach can be so helpful.

"I'll Jump with You"

Many of us can imagine a big leap we'd love to take. But sometimes, we could all use some help to make it happen—because the big leap feels like it might just be a plunge off the cliff.

Maybe that means someone to say, "I dare you." Maybe it means someone to say, "I'll jump with you." Maybe you need someone to actually give you a shove.

Sometimes, we could all use some help because the big leap feels like it might just be a plunge off the cliff.

Why is that? Because it's hard for us to push ourselves with the same intensity that someone else can push us. I'll mention another example from Tai Chi. If I always train by myself, and I don't have a teacher, my development is going to be probably one quarter of my potential. A teacher is willing to push me harder than I will push myself, to hold my feet to the fire when I would jump back. My Tai Chi teacher has pushed me to potential I didn't even know I had.

You can benefit quite a bit from having that person behind you who doesn't let you step back. Because otherwise, how long are you going to stay on the cliff? You'll always give yourself a break, an excuse not to take the leap, so it helps to have someone who *won't* give you a break.

Eventually, you're gonna step off because you have nowhere else to go. So you need that person there, making sure you don't betray yourself and what you really want—so you jump at the right time, for the right reason, in the right direction.

Still, it's scary. What if you encounter failure? Bad news: You probably will! But get over it, because there's good news too: It's only from trying and failing that you can find out what the real barriers are. And—whether you're the coachee, the coach, or the organization cultivating better leaders—you have to confront those barriers. You need to take action to get under the surface of those barriers. That's the only way to move them aside and shoot upward again. That's what the next chapter is all about.

Coach: How about getting started with one of these approaches?

1. Start now. Don't wait until everything is perfect and you feel ready. That will be too late—or never.

2. Look for your intrinsic or internal motivation. Ignore the naysayers.

3. Start from where you are. Take the easy step. The goal is to get going.

4. Name the first step and commit to it. Don't get distracted.

5. Articulate your fears and debunk each one. Likely, most are about projected (imagined) failure, not reality.

6. Gather some cheerleaders for yourself. Everyone can use some support.

7. Trust yourself, that you can handle whatever happens.

Coach: What will work to get you going?

5

Break Down

> **Coach: I thought we agreed you were going to try a new approach. What happened?**
>
> *The more I thought about it, the more I worried that it would fail.*
>
> **Coach: So, what's your alternative?**
>
> *Can't I just keep doing what always worked before?*

There's a perfectly understandable reason why both experienced and aspiring leaders resist change. It's so commonplace, in fact, that entire training and human resource departments—and even entire organizations—struggle with how to address this problem. Fear of failure is part of it. But really the wall of resistance is grounded in the fact that the familiar is much more comforting. We all have a tendency to do what we've done before. It worked last time, so why wouldn't it work now? If your whole career is predicated on knowing what works, why would you try something new?

If your whole career is predicated on knowing what works, why would you try something new?

Rationally, we all know the answer to that. Refusal to experiment and a failure-averse mindset are innovation killers. Moreover, even if you're content to stand pat, the rest of the work world is going to keep evolving whether you like it or not. Doing the same old thing eventually means falling behind, so even when you've punched that first hole in the wall of resistance, that's not enough. You have to keep working to tear it down. You need to keep experimenting.

If we know all of that rationally, then we also know that in real life our behavior isn't strictly rational. The instinct to avoid the risk of failure and the shock of change and the comfort of clinging to the familiar are all emotionally powerful patterns. They can overwhelm the rational part of us. I've seen it happen. In fact, I've even experienced it myself.

When I quit my steady job at a training firm to start my own coaching practice in the mid 1990s, I wasn't afraid of failure—even when it seemed like everyone thought I was crazy. What are you doing? they said. Are you kidding me? Your income's gonna drop significantly! It was true that what I was already doing (working for a consulting firm) was going perfectly fine. But I knew this was the right change, the right risk, and the best path to get what I really really wanted. And over the next two decades I built my practice up to something that made a very good living for me.

The truth is that I got quite comfortable. I was so comfortable that when I was offered a chance to make another big change—a daring experiment—I dismissed it.

A client of mine who I had coached off and on over several years was starting a new company and wanted me to be part of it. "Come in with me at the beginning," he urged.

While I had embraced experimentation and risk when I quit that training job, this time I preferred to stay comfortable. "No," I told him, "I don't think I want to do that." His new company was an early virtual-reality start-up, which sounded interesting but was hardly my area of expertise. Besides, I had been thriving independently for 20 years, doing work I really enjoyed. This opportunity would mean I worked inside a company. "I'm used to being the outside person," I told him. "I don't think I want to go inside." Plus, I was working on a book.

I never did finish that book, of course, because I ended up joining the start-up. I'll explain what changed my mind, and how it all worked out, but first I want to go a little deeper on why backsliding and complacency are so common, and how to avoid them.

Persistence over Time

In a way, this chapter is about failure—but that's only part of the point. The term *break down* has two meanings. One is quite negative: another way, in fact, of describing a failure. But the other is very different. To "break down" a problem or a challenge or a situation is to consider it from a calm perspective, analyze it, learn from it. This more forward-looking version of the term is the one I'll ultimately focus on. We can extract useful lessons from breaking down a failure, but also from breaking down a missed opportunity, a fear, a cautious hesitation.

> To "break down" a problem or a challenge or a situation is to consider it from a calm perspective, analyze it, learn from it.

To make a real change, you have to experiment, and sometimes that doesn't work out. It's an inevitable part of the process. But when we meet failure, or even the chance of failure, most of us recoil and return to familiar patterns. We don't really strategize and keep going in new ways. And while it may sound counterintuitive, failure is often hardest on people who have a long track record of success. Instead of providing a sort of armor or at least perspective, a success-filled trajectory can make people more fragile and resistant. A single misstep can seriously undermine their confidence.

There's a related idea in Tai Chi: persistence over time. The people who do the best with Tai Chi are not necessarily the "naturals" who seem to get off to a strong start. When those naturals start to encounter challenges, they struggle, and often fall off altogether. The people who succeed in the longer run are the ones who have to work hard at things from the start and have been persistent over a long period of time. They just keep going;

they take the missteps as part of the process. A related concept is called "investing in loss." The idea is that without losing, there is no learning. In fact, loss is where the best learning happens.

> *It takes loss for us to deeply comprehend what it takes to win.*

It takes loss for us to deeply comprehend what it takes to win.

It can be the same in a career. Often, someone who has risen to a leadership role has gotten used to a certain degree of success, maybe even to doing certain things easily. It's a shock when they reach a level where that's no longer true. Consider a student who is a star at their high school and goes to a prestigious college, only to discover that all their new peers are at least as smart as they are. People think that being a winner early in life sets you up for the long haul. Actually, winning early in life can end up making you think everything will come easily, which often turns out to be a limiting mindset.

I've coached a number of executives who got to their late 40s or 50s without absorbing a big failure. And without that experience there can be a kind of internal strength that's missing: They didn't have that direct experience of facing and overcoming adversity. A couple of such clients ended up having a big failure while I was coaching them, and it was very difficult for them to get past it because they just didn't have any practice with failing and learning. They thought they'd lost it all, that their careers were over.

What makes this extra complicated is that these were C-suite executives or even CEOs. So it's not about their being too passive by nature, just hoping for the best. These are people used to taking action and succeeding. So when that success pattern gets interrupted, a defense mechanism kicks in. They had to get past the defensiveness. And that can be tricky.

Feeling Failure

One memorable example of how devastating failure can be to someone with a track record of success involved a senior executive in his 40s who signed on for coaching because he had switched to a new company with a different culture, and he wanted to make the adjustment as smooth as possible. He wasn't in crisis; he was being proactive and ambitious, just as he'd always been. Then, a few sessions into the engagement, he experienced a significant failure: a huge deal he was negotiating collapsed. He had been working on it, leading a large team, for months. It was why he was hired for the role. In fact it was not only a primary focus, it was his key performance indicator. He was sure he was going to get fired.

This was devastating to him, because he had gotten all the way to that age without ever having failed, and thus without ever having *learned* from failure. He got straight A's in high school, thrived at an Ivy League college, enjoyed a great career and a charmed life. So this one setback hit him really hard. Suddenly it was like he was no longer playing to win; he was playing to *not lose*, which is rarely a good strategy.

Getting him back on track was a process that took several months. Working through a failure doesn't always take that long (he was a tough case) but the arc of the process is always similar.

First, we have to go through the person's emotional reaction. Often there's a lot of verbiage from the coachee in this scenario as they extensively recap everything that happened. What I do is listen to this and take the next step: I name their feelings.

"Oh, so you're completely shocked?"

"So you feel terrified?"

"You're worried about how your boss will respond?"

"Your confidence is shaken?"

I'm simply naming their emotions, helping them to *feel* their failure. This is a really important step. For starters, leaders often lack any language for emotion about failure, because that's never been relevant to their successful career trajectory. Many people are trained in the traditional, old-school framework that emotions don't belong at work. So they try to hide them, or rationalize their experience with "logic" that blots out feelings. This rarely works. Most important, if you don't *name* the emotion that is happening, then it's as if you're avoiding and resisting it. When you do this, you lack clarity about the problem or challenge you need to resolve.

Emotions are like ocean waves. They wash up and wash back, wash up and wash back. If you don't acknowledge them, eventually a wave washes up and doesn't recede, so you can actually end up drowning in it. Now, this is not therapy, and we're not going to proceed to explore the deep roots of the coachee's emotional response; that's something they can pursue elsewhere. All I do is name those feelings, in the present, and that lets the waters recede.

The point is to get the problem out in the open and face it. They often seem relieved to just have it stated. "So you are deeply disappointed in yourself?" "Oh God, yes—that's exactly it!"

Sometimes it's more complicated. The person may describe their feeling as sadness, but as they tell me their story I'm able to figure out something else might be going on, and as an outside observer it's easier for me to not only notice but *name* that emotion: "It kind of sounds to me like you're not just sad, but hurt. You feel betrayed by someone you thought was an ally." Suddenly, the whole conversation changes. We can talk about what that other person might have been thinking, what their motivation (and indeed *their* emotions) might have been.

Or sometimes my summary is off, and they'll correct me and, in that process, end up naming the emotion themselves: "Oh no, I wasn't shocked, but I felt totally let down."

How ever it plays out, naming the emotion allows a different kind of thinking, that is truly unblocked and no longer covered by the emotion.

Once we work through this, and the water recedes a little bit, the next move is to take a step back and assess the *real* impact of this setback. Let's return to the example of the senior executive who had recently started at a new company and was coping with his first real failure. It was pretty clear that it wasn't going to cost him his job, and once he accepted that, he got out of the defensive survival mode he'd gotten stuck in.

Even in the worst-case scenario, the problem people face in a coaching situation isn't literally life or death. Working through that reality is the next step. I might ask, "So let's say they do fire you. What then? Maybe you can finally take a vacation. Maybe you'll find a better opportunity." Once you get out of survival mode, then you can focus on *what you learned* from this failure, rather than obsessing about its consequences and existential meaning.

What did you learn about yourself? What did you learn about failure? What did you learn for next time? That's the part of the process that builds resilience, and wisdom. Breaking down a failure is what makes it possible to see beyond that failure, and focus on the future again.

> *Breaking down a failure is what makes it possible to see beyond that failure, and focus on the future again.*

Blame and Courage

The specific details in the way different individuals confront these moments of challenge or failure obviously vary quite a bit. Sometimes they want to blame someone who they can be mad at. Occasionally, that's been me! I had one client who was working through a failure, and when I tried to get him to confront it and take new steps to move on, he got so mad that he stomped out of our session and didn't contact or respond to me for two months. My suggestion had been a tough one, that he forgive the person he felt had wronged him. I worried it would be my first completely failed engagement!

But finally he got in touch and said, "I did what you suggested. It took me two months but I did it. I'm ready to talk again." This was hard internal work, and even when he saw my point, he felt he needed to do that work on his own. When he returned, he made fast progress toward repairing that relationship and several others. He had learned a larger lesson about blame—and was quickly promoted.

In a completely different context, I worked with a CEO who showed up at one of our sessions and said his board had asked him to resign. It sounded like he was going to do it, and I was shocked. "What? Why would you do that?" I asked him. "Why don't you go back to them with a plan about how you are going to succeed?" He hadn't talked about leaving the company at all. He was just being impacted by what he perceived as a failure.

His immediate reaction was, "I'll never be able to convince them." He sounded defeated.

I suggested that this was a moment to think about what he really wanted. Did he still want to be the CEO? Did he want to grow with the company? Maybe he was ready to get out? Maybe he'd given this enough of his life? We had our first conversation on a Wednesday. That Friday he went to the ocean, cleared his head, and thought about what he really wanted. The following Monday he called me and said, "Here's my plan for going back to the board. I'm not leaving." And it worked.

Unlike some clients, this guy is very resilient by nature. He's been through a lot of hardship in his life, so he was able to zero in on what he really wanted pretty quickly: *I want this company to succeed, and if I leave it isn't going to succeed.* Then, he just got down to business and did it.

For others it takes longer to work through all these steps I've just described. But despite those differences, the broad coaching approach is always the same: confronting risks, breaking down failures, deciding what you really want. I've seen it take hours, and I've seen it take years.

It always takes courage. It takes deep courage to do the thing that you really want.

It always takes courage. It takes deep courage to do the thing that you really want.

Breaking (Failure) Down

Just getting to the point of saying, "Okay, I failed" is actually the hardest part.

People and organizations have a lot of ways to avoid thinking about failure. Failure is disappointing, so it's much easier to rationalize it by making it someone else's fault or chalking it up to circumstances beyond your control. Just getting to the point of saying, "Okay, I failed" is actually the hardest part.

But once you get there, it's not over. The next step is to take that failure apart and question what your part was in the failure. Sure, there were other actors, a bigger context, and so on. But what was *your* role in what went wrong?

Then, take it a step further by asking, "Is there anything I can do right now to improve the situation?" If there isn't anything you can do to correct the problem, then consider what you can learn from the experience and use going forward.

These are the questions to spend time on, because now it's about pushing through to the other side. For a coach, that means helping the coachee see that they're going to be okay. You took a risk and it didn't work. Your ego took a hit, and internally you're feeling that failure. Externally, maybe you hurt your reputation in the short term because everyone knows you failed with this experiment. But you didn't get fired! You still have this job. The worst outcome didn't happen, which is a sign that the people around you still think you have skills and potential. So now, what are you gonna do?

But What If I *Do* Get Fired?

Now I'm not saying the worst-case scenario never happens. People really do get fired. That's why part of the broad coaching approach must always include looking that worst-case scenario in the eye. The goal is to stop obsessing about it, but to see it, in proper perspective.

When I first started my coaching practice, and everyone was telling me I was crazy, I had doubts and fears of my own. I was a single parent. What if I couldn't pay my mortgage and feed my child? I talked to my sister and asked her: If I got in really bad trouble, could we come live with you? I'm very lucky because she said yes. Although neither one of us thought this would happen, it allowed me to feel I had a backup plan. The worst possible outcome—being in a homeless shelter with my kid—is not going to happen. It gave me a kind of personal permission to forge ahead.

That's an extreme example, but the point is to establish a kind of floor. Because in real time, it's very easy to imagine there *is* no floor, no safety net, no bottom. I've worked with CEOs who got fired and believed their world had ended. The truth, as I remind them, is that they'll likely land another CEO position. Once you're in the CEO club, you can't get out (unless you wind up in jail). This is true with pretty much any role that entails having gained a certain level of expertise. It might take a year to find something comparable, but that level of expertise and skill is a kind of floor. What's important is to keep perspective: Rule out the worst-case scenario. Maybe, like me, you need to create that floor yourself. But it's there to reassure you. (I never had to go live with my sister, even though she wished I had moved in anyway.)

It's worth noting here that it's better not to wait for a pivotal moment of crisis but, rather, to create that floor proactively. I once gave a talk to a group of executives who were all high-powered women with impressive educational backgrounds and jobs at top-end firms. In the Q&A afterward, I kept hearing variations on: "When I go into the boardroom, or some key executive meeting, I can't say what I really want to say, because I'm afraid I'd get fired."

And I replied, "Wait a minute. You're a graduate of Stanford or Harvard (or whatever) and a veteran of Google or Apple (or whatever). If you get fired, you're going to get another job! Why do you *want* to stay at this job if you can't have influence and people aren't listening to you? Why *wouldn't* you take the risk?"

You need to establish the floor, because without it, the fear of the worst-case scenario stops you from doing the thing that you really want.

Leave It Behind

With the client I mentioned earlier, who got so deep into a successful career without a serious failure, the process was difficult. He did not get fired, but it took him four to six months to get over his first failure. Once he did, he saw that he could fail and get past it, and it just transformed his leadership. He wasn't playing not to lose anymore. He was playing to win, because he knew he could survive a failure.

But it wasn't just that. He also had a lot more compassion. After making it through a difficult situation himself, he understood how fear of failure can get in the way, and that made him a much better leader.

> *He was playing to win, because he knew he could survive a failure.*

Instead of waves crashing over you, they recede. Now it's over. It's done. You have to let it go.

Here's a story I sometimes tell clients who are trying to break down their failures and break through to whatever comes next. It's about a sculptor. Well, it's about a bunch of sculptors, but one in particular.

The story happens in medieval times, and involves a king seeking a royal sculptor. Half a dozen artists are given the chance to compete and ordered to bring a new work to the castle for the king to judge. It's a long journey, at least a week, with each artist traveling in a cart pulled by a donkey.

Before leaving home, each sculptor makes a preliminary work, although none of the artists are really satisfied. On one sculpture the hands aren't quite right; on another the head isn't in proportion. All of them recognize that something's just off. And so they go to sleep thinking about their failure and they dream about whatever's not right.

The next morning, five of the six loaded their failed sculptures onto their carts, just in case it could prove useful, or if they can't do better next time. The sixth sculptor, however, says, "Eh, that one wasn't good, and I think I see the flaw. I'll just leave it here, and do better on the next try."

Each sculptor travels for part of the day, then stops and repeats the process. Everybody makes another sculpture, but nobody is satisfied. The same sculptor leaves his attempt behind, but the others add it to their carts. This happens every day.

By the fourth day, five of the carts are sagging under the weight of all the subpar work; the donkeys are spent. Over the next couple of days, the carts break down. Some lose wheels and others collapse under the weight of big monuments of failure.

By the seventh day, only one artist makes it to the castle. His cart is empty because he didn't insist on carrying all of his missteps with him. On the castle grounds, he proceeds to make a new sculpture. Having learned from his past missteps, it's his best work yet. Of course, he gets hired as the royal sculptor. Not only did he leave his failures behind, but he also applied what he had learned from them to help himself improve.

What Will Be Successful Next?

Learn from your failures and leave them behind. Don't take the easy route. Keep going toward what you really really want. Be resilient. Don't fall back.

It's also true for developing leaders, and it's true for the organizations supporting them. In fact, individuals and organizations face the exact same pattern. There's external change, but when a new experiment doesn't go as expected, it's easiest to just go back to what used to work.

The idea that "this used to work, so let's keep doing it" may be even more deeply ingrained in organizations than it is in individuals. For a company, it's always going to feel like a giant pain and a lot of work to try to figure out something new; not only is it uncertain to work, it's a big lift to find out.

The idea that "this used to work, so let's keep doing it" may be even more deeply ingrained in organizations than it is in individuals.

I'll give you two examples of areas where organizations have resisted change, even as the world changes around them.

The first example is very current. During the pandemic, lots of companies were forced to deal with employees working remotely. This was popular with some employees, who wanted to make this option permanent. Some employers adjusted, while others insisted on a return to the office. There's also a third category, which to me is the most fascinating: the companies that *sort of* accommodate remote work—but instead of really adjusting, have decided that they need to implement various remote surveillance tools, like software that monitors keystrokes. Evidently, they just can't let go of the idea that productivity is something that has to be monitored in real time, by tracking hours spent "working," rather than investigating their ideas around employee trust and creating new opportunities for employees. It's a strange response to an opportunity for real change, and a crystallization of a failure to let go. Other companies ask employees to be *hybrid* workers, requiring them to come to the office some number of days a week. I have heard many hybrid workers complain that when they did put the effort and time going into the office, no one else was there. They were still working by themselves on video meetings, now from an empty office instead of from home. Needless to say, this has not been a successful solution for employees.

The second example is more evergreen but taps into more fundamental ways of thinking about leadership development itself. It's about the traditional idea of "mentoring," and why some organizations remain stuck on an antiquated version of its utility. Specifically, some have embraced it more tightly than ever in response to the steady spread of coaching as a development strategy.

There's nothing wrong with mentoring, but it's fundamentally different from coaching. Mentoring is having someone who has already done something tell you how they did it. That can be useful, but it's a very different approach than coaching, which is

*Coaching is a methodol-
ogy for looking out
ahead and figuring out
what's going to be suc-
cessful next.*

helping you figure out how *you* are going to achieve some goal in the future, not how *someone else* achieved various goals in the past. In a sense, mentoring can encourage looking back, emulating what was previously successful. Coaching is a methodology for looking out ahead and figuring out what's going to be successful next.

Needless to say, you can have (and learn from) a mentor *and* a coach. But the mentor dynamic is so familiar to both organizations and up-and-coming leaders that it can become a trap.

Think about what people look for in a mentor. One thing they look for is someone who has done their job before, and who therefore knows what they "should" do. Second, they look for a powerful person that they think is going to be a champion for them within the organization. But that is actually different than mentoring, so often the mentee is disappointed when that person doesn't put them up for new positions or try to influence others on their behalf or otherwise promote their career. That's misunderstanding of the role of the mentor. Many mentors can see the relationship as an obligation or a sharing of their own success. There isn't an agreement to promote the mentee in their network or into new roles. Their own reputation is at stake. So they can share what worked for them in the past, maybe the present, and can give advice. But often this relationship is not about the needs of the mentee.

Coaching is the opposite. It is not designed as a forum for coaches to share their own experiences. It's designed as a forum for a coach to be invested in the coachee's experience.

Mentoring is not wrong in and of itself. Why not talk to people who have done your job previously and hear how they thought about it? It can be good for expanding the idea set. What you really need, beyond that, is guidance to help you figure out which of those ideas are a fit for you, in the current environment. So while the mentor is giving information, they're not necessarily helping sort the information, apply the information, fit the information into who the aspiring leader is and their current situation. There's generally no particular rigor to mentoring programs. The relationship often peters out fairly early on.

And yet, mentoring programs are still applied everywhere. Because they're easy! They're easy in part *because* there's no rigor; anybody who wants to be a mentor can be a mentor. So an organization can set up and deploy a mentoring system in a week, and feel like that's a response to an internal development challenge. But there's no guarantee that this system will be useful, and there certainly aren't a lot of analytics around mentoring.

That's because it's an example of a practice, and a supposed solution, that's not really about figuring out what works for the future. It's about repeating what's worked in the past. Mentoring has been a low-cost development tool for organizations since the last century. It sticks because there is value to it. And at its best, it can be invaluable. Mentoring just can't take the place of the kind of transformative development employees can get from coaching. It can help up-and-coming leaders see that seasoned leaders have failures too and live to tell the tale. When mentors can also talk about their own process overcoming failure and share their learning from their experience, now there is bigger impact. For mentors to share their darkest moment, there needs to be trust in the relationship. Matching mentors based on functional area is fine for basic info sharing. For senior leaders to share their own learning and development, matching for deep relationship is a better way. At Sounding Board, we think coaching and mentoring are complementary, so we offer mentoring software that can run along side coaching and be matched and measured in a similar vein. This means using our same widely successful relationship matching algorithm (with additional filters) and our leader profile, goal tools, and leadership roadmap

Mentoring just can't take the place of the kind of transformative development employees can get from coaching.

tracking tools for mentoring as well. Hopefully this adds some focus and rigor to mentoring programs and creates deep, long-lasting relationships that provide more value and satisfaction for both mentor and mentee.

Break Through

Sometimes coaching is just constantly stating the obvious. That might not sound important, but it is. Often "the obvious" is exactly what we need to hear, because we've totally lost track of it in the moment. As my old co-trainer said regularly, "Common sense isn't common practice." We *need* to hear a neutral observer say, "You know, you said you wanted to do something new. And yet, you're doing the same thing you did before. But somehow you're hoping for a different outcome." Obvious. But it helps to hear someone observe and name this.

Essentially, the goal is to make that sort of disconnect visible. Early in the arc of a coaching engagement, it's all about helping identify a new mindset, new ways of thinking that lead to new actions. But then the focus has to shift in part to help avoid falling back to old patterns. Under stress, human nature is programmed to fall back to what is already known. In the heat of battle, for example, when competitively pushing hands in the Tai Chi school, it's easy to keep using the same push over and over, whether it succeeds or not. It's the most familiar action under stress.

When that happens, it's a coach's job to say: "Wait a minute, how are you thinking about that? Isn't that the same old thinking? I thought you were operating off this new thinking that you were so excited about." It's obvious, but you have to bring it to the coachee's attention, "Oh no, you slipped back!"

And this is why, somewhere around the middle phase of the coaching engagement, it becomes crucial not to just experiment with new ideas and behaviors, but to accept and embrace the missteps and even failures that inevitably happen. So now you've tried a few things, and it's not working as well as you would hope; you really wanted to get it right on your first try, and you're not. That's bringing up all your issues around success and failure that you have to work through. You have to break down those issues, too.

Break down sounds like a harsh term—but it's necessary. You have to go through the break *down* before you can have the break *through*.

That's certainly how it worked out for the client I was describing earlier. It took him a while to break down his first real brush with failure, but he ended up just killing it after that. Once he figured out how to get through failing, he was unstoppable.

> *You have to go through the break* down *before you can have the* break *through.*

The Path of Action

This brings me back to that other earlier example of a person who resisted change because the ways that "always worked" were just more comfortable. Sometimes resisting change isn't a reaction to a failure, but to a fear, a hesitation, a reluctance to take a risk that *might* lead to failure—or that the change just seems impossible to visualize. Those challenges also need to be "broken down."

When that former client offered me a role in his start-up, I couldn't even imagine it. That was part my resistance—not really being able to picture what this would be like. Why would I work in an office when I had been working in my home office for 20 years? Why would I take on a boss when I was my own boss most of my career? It just didn't make any sense to me.

But my former client was so smart. He had after all been a coaching client, off and on, for years. So he knew exactly what to do. The path forward in the face of resistance is often a series of small steps that minimizes the coachees' resistance and works them up to taking much bigger leap. He is a master salesperson and knew the value of getting a series of small yeses to move me past my objections to the big yes.

He coaxed me one little step at a time. First it was, "Oh, just come meet my co-founder and let's have a drink." Well, okay, fine.

"Hey, come in, see our office!" Oh, all right.

"Why don't you come and meet the lead investor?" Sure, what could it hurt?

After each of these events he'd ask, "Can you join now? Will you join now?" And I'd say No, no, no.

He didn't stop. He slowly walked me down the path of action. And he just kept going. Finally we had the conversation about how this all could really work, which of course, totally enticed me. It was a big-vision conversation. I was starting to picture it.

He kept wearing me down. He threw in the traditional pitches, too: better salary treatment, stock options, the works.

But all along the way, I was resisting. It was just uncertainty. This would be really different than anything I'd done before. I'd worked independently, and in a completely different industry, for 20 years. But he finally got me to the point where I was asking myself, what do I really, really want?

Figuring out what you really want is not a one-and-done event. It's something that has to be asked and answered over and over.

This is part of the advancement, revisiting this question I thought I had already answered. I had clarity on it when I completed my private coaching practice. But now a new possibility had surfaced that I had not considered. Figuring out what you really want is not a one-and-done event. It's something that has to be asked and answered over and over.

In my current role at Sounding Board, I ask a version of this question many times a day. In meetings, when the conversation gets complicated or off track, I ask "What do you really want to get from this meeting?" or "What do you really want for this project?" When I'm having career conversations with employees, I ask, "What do you want for yourself over the next three to five years?" When there is a conflict, I ask, "What do you each really want?" Surprisingly, the conflicting individuals often want something very close to the same thing. The disagreement is about the path to that outcome; now there can be a productive conversation on how to get there.

In my case, facing this potential change, I was a little in a fog. Is this what I want to do? Do I want to keep working independently? Do I want to have the experience of working with this team in this new industry? Do I want to do the hard, hard work of actually starting a company? I don't know if I even know how to start a company. But do I want to?

And then, after our next conversation (I think it was our sixth), I said something like, "Okay, fine." He said: "You said Yes!" And for a second I almost denied it. But it was true. I'd signed on.

That, however, wasn't the end of the challenge. Remember how when I left my steady job at a training company to build my coaching practice, everyone said I was crazy? Well, that happened again. "Why are you stopping now? You've spent 20 years building a successful practice!"

But that was just it: I realized that while I'd been telling myself "I've been doing this for 20 years," I thought I was reassuring myself. In reality, I was challenging myself—I needed to do something different.

Still, I admit, my trepidation didn't go away when I made my decision. I went into my new role suspecting that, despite everything, I was going to hate it . . . and I ended up loving it.

I loved building a company. I loved building a team. I loved being on the inside, with all those people and all the exchange of ideas about how to grow and how to create the product and how to create the structure. To be honest I was totally shocked how much I loved it. There was this long walkway to the office, with no windows, and I distinctly remember walking down the hallway and just feeling so happy to be there—and how amazed I was about that. I had a really great experience with that company.

And that's despite the fact that—here's the kicker—that company died. It went from zero to post-series A funding, but it never quite clicked in the marketplace of the time, the investors had competing visions, and it didn't work out.

But I learned so much, taking the whole Silicon Valley iconic journey from the garage to an office, the funding adventures, making payroll, the full start-up experience. The business had nothing to do with coaching at all, or training, or management. What it taught me was how to grow a company and what that whole adventure was.

And what it *really* taught me was just how much I like growing stuff: people, leaders, businesses, children. I really, really enjoyed the process of growing a company. I used all of what I knew about leadership development and coaching to do that. So what at the time felt like a total change in direction, a decision that was largely intuition, actually built on and extended my expertise. Not long afterwards, the opportunity to co-found Sounding Board came along, I was ready in a way I never could have been without this experience. It would turn out to be a match made in heaven.

But of course I couldn't have known that at the time. I've looked back since and thought: "Oh, I see why I needed to take that risk—and even absorb that setback of the company failing." I needed to do something I hadn't done before. Sure, I had coached a lot of people in startups. I coached VCs, founders, CEOs, that whole crowd. It was time for me to see if I could *do* all the stuff I'd been coaching people on, to test whether it actually works. It was time for me to see if I could walk my own talk. And what I learned was that I could.

The most important way I walked my talk was to let go of the comfortable way of doing things, risk and cope with failure, and not only figure out but pursue what I really really wanted. It truly was a big leap.

The Choice Is Yours

I've seen versions of this same journey in countless coaching clients. They don't simply worry that some new experiment or risk isn't going to work out. They are convinced that it won't. That's the only outcome they can imagine. "I don't see how this is going to be better than doing what's always worked for me before," they'll insist.

And then they finally get convinced to try something new. And lo and behold: "Oh, my God, that actually worked way better than I thought!"

The bottom line is that all of this is about making a choice. Not doing things because "that's how it used to be done," or "that's how I identified myself," or "that's all I know"—it's a choice. You are choosing to stand pat and hope for the best, even if that very strategy is what's left you dissatisfied and curious about change.

I grew up hearing the saying "You've made your bed, now you have to lie in it." But when I got out on my own, I realized that wasn't true. I could remake my bed, or not make it at all, or make up an entirely new bed. It was all up to me.

You can rechoose anytime you want. And it's the new choice that changes everything.

Coach: Here Are Some Ideas for How to Learn from Your Failures

1. **Accept your feelings and emotions.** Failure can be disappointing, devastating, irritating, interesting, inspiring. Remember you are not "a failure"! Something didn't work out or you had a setback. It's temporary: That does not mean your life/career is over. Realize you *have* to fail to reach your highest potential.

2. **Turn off the "what if" voice in your head.** Instead, create a backup plan and establish a floor for yourself. This will ground you in reality so you don't spiral into thoughts of the worst-case scenario.

3. **Get back out there.** Isolating yourself or giving up is really the only way to truly fail. Take the right amount of responsibility for things that are within your control.

4. **List what you've learned from failure.** It should be a long list. Look forward, and ask yourself: "What can I do differently next time?" Experience really is the best teacher! Failure builds character, wisdom, compassion, creativity, motivation, skills.

5. **Let it go and move on to the next challenge.** You're likely more resilient and better prepared for similar challenges.

   Coach: Which of these ideas can help you right now?

Breakthrough

I tried using a new skill I'm really excited about, but it didn't pan out.

Coach: Do you still feel like that skill is valuable?

Absolutely. I know it's going to help me. That's why I was anxious to try it.

Coach: Then maybe the problem was that you used a good skill but in the wrong situation.

Many managers and aspiring leaders—and even many seasoned leaders—struggle with the idea of leaving behind old habits and making new choices. Or, actually, they don't struggle with the idea; they struggle with the practice.

Most can understand (especially in the current, constantly shifting work and business environment) that success requires fresh decisions, new actions, and novel solutions. Unfortunately, few have been trained or developed or guided to execute on that core insight. That's why, as we saw in Chapter 5, even ambitious and accomplished individuals and organizations so often backslide into familiar modes of thinking and behavior. Even after doing the hard work of breaking down what's holding them back, they can have trouble breaking *through* to a new way of doing things.

Coaching can be particularly helpful in achieving those breakthroughs, because it takes a more nuanced and individualized approach to leadership development. By the midpoint of a coaching engagement, the coachee is often actively experimenting with new ideas, but still tentative about committing to them. That's part of the process of getting to breakthroughs.

Here's a helpful framework to think about the challenge, and its solution. There are two modes of development: the horizontal and the vertical (Figure 6.1). Both are important, but one tends to get way more emphasis than the other. And that's a problem.

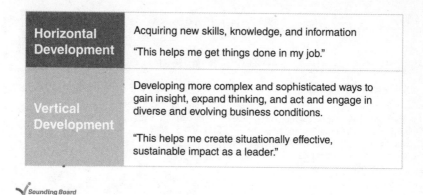

Horizontal Development	Acquiring new skills, knowledge, and information "This helps me get things done in my job."
Vertical Development	Developing more complex and sophisticated ways to gain insight, expand thinking, and act and engage in diverse and evolving business conditions. "This helps me create situationally effective, sustainable impact as a leader."

Sounding Board

FIGURE 6.1 A comparison of horizontal and vertical development.

Horizontal development basically refers to acquiring and developing particular skills—the tactical skill sets you need for your job, or to qualify for the job you aspire to. It's linear and logical, an approach that reflects an almost industrial-era mindset (Figure 6.2). And of course the thoughtful and guided acquisition of skills is important! That's why every competent development,

What is horizontal development?

Horizontal development typically focuses on developing skills, models, and abilities from a tactical perspective. This dimension of leader development has been the focus for the last 40+ years.

Horizontal development is often most useful when:

- Challenges and their resolutions are clearly defined

- The problems leaders face occur in predictable or familiar environments or conditions

- There is a simple formula for success

Sounding Board

FIGURE 6.2 Horizontal development.

What is vertical development?

Vertical development is a more emergent form of development. It focuses on an individual's unique growth developing increasing socioemotional, sensory, and cognitive sophistication and capacity.

 Sounding Board

Vertical development helps leaders to:

- Respond effectively in systems of increasing complexity

- Understand and create from divergent perspectives and cross-cultural relationships

- Be present, self-regulating, flexible, and courageous

FIGURE 6.3 Vertical development.

training, and HR program or department revolves around some version of horizontal-style skill acquisition, and has been since the 1960s or before.

But vertical development, which is much less common, is crucial, too. Probably more so than ever. Vertical development is a way of thinking (Figure 6.3). If horizontal development is about acquiring *skills*, vertical development is about building *capacity*—namely, capacity, as a leader, for dealing with a nonpredictive environment while maintaining composure, judgment, and presence.

I'll say more later about what I mean by "building capacity," but in short it refers to a leader's ability to discern which skills to deploy,

What you can do is develop the capacities and skills that can help you address whatever the future turns out to be.

and how to deploy them, in which situations. Vertical development is about building an ability to deal with the unpredictable. It is distinctly future-oriented. Because in the modern work environment—as the pandemic forcefully reminded everyone—practically the only thing we can be certain of is that you can't know the future. But what you can do is develop the capacities and skills that can help you address whatever the future turns out to be.

Learning by Sparring

This approach is the cornerstone of coaching. It's not about training to obtain a preset list of skills. It's about developing the awareness to respond appropriately to unpredicted challenges.

What's the situation? What skills do you have? Which of those would be the best to apply here? When and at what level of intensity? The coach helps the individual figure out the best application of those skills.

But really that's just in the short term. Longer term, coaching helps the leader or aspiring leader to build the capacity to figure out the answers to those questions on their own. That's the capacity building at the heart of vertical development. In Chapter 3, I referred to a coach as a "thinking partner." That's because coaches do not tell their coachees what to do. Instead, they help people think through how to apply skills in a variety of individual situations. What happens over time is that coachees start to develop that judgment on their own.

To borrow an idea from the martial arts, you can think of the process as akin to sparring. In each match, you're dealing with a relatively straightforward challenge, by using a specific skill or skills. But to reach that black-belt level, you may have to demonstrate that you can fend off multiple opponents at the same time, requiring different skills deployed in different ways, with little room for hesitation. The point is that you gradually develop the ability to deal with more and more complexity and unpredictability—both from the experience of doing it and the conversation around those experiences.

So when coaching revisits past experiences, it's not to dwell on what used to work. Instead, it's like studying the tape of a past match, and drawing lessons from it: You relied on this skill here; a better application would have been to apply another skill that you also have. (Or, perhaps there's a specific new skill you need to acquire—vertical and horizontal development should complement each other; more on that later.) Of course there's no game tape in a work setting, but talking through different scenarios can play a similar role.

What matters is that the process is always ultimately forward looking. Sparring is never about reliving the last bout. It's about anticipating the next one.

Why We Get Stuck on the Horizontal

To me, the benefits of this approach have been obvious for decades; that's why I embraced coaching in the first place. But in recent years, it's become increasingly accepted that responding to the work world of today requires a new kind of agility and flexibility—which is precisely the point of vertical leadership development. And yet, when I talk to many training, management, and HR professionals, I'm surprised by how many find vertical development to be a novel, cutting-edge approach—someone even called it "the tip of the spear."

Maybe I shouldn't be surprised. In part, our tendency to revert to the familiar is rooted in human psychology, which feeds all too easily into *organizational* psychology. Horizontal development took hold in the first place partly because for many decades the future was more predictable (or seemed to be). There was a consensus about what was coming next, and what skills everyone needed. Industrial-era workers and managers had a sense of what would happen the next day, the next month, and next year, right up to the time they would retire. Sure, everyone expected some bumps, but there was a fundamental certainty about where things were going and what we needed to do to get there.

This resulted in the focus on horizontal development, detailed systems for enabling the acquisition of consistent skills or knowledge. This could be coding, writing, or project management. Or it could be interpersonal skills or skills related to leadership. More recently, the idea of "upskilling" came into vogue, referring to the acquisition of newer or more specific skills. But this was still predicated on the faith in learning skills that could be applied in a predictable, homogenous, standard environment. So even now, organizations continue to get better and better at building training courses that teach skills but with an emphasis on gaining the skill—not on applying it.

One reason so many organizations remain primarily focused on horizontal development is that it's easier to do. Aside from traditional training programs, now there are a plethora of learning platforms, all focused on skill development. The upskill phenomenon has only boosted this focus, fueled by the idea that robots or automation will take over lesser-skilled jobs, so ever-bigger chunks of the workforce need to acquire more advanced skills.

And while that's a reasonable response to a legitimate concern, it's not enough for developing leadership. Functional skills are not enough to help you run or grow a company, a group, a team, or a division. You have to attain a broader view on things to be able to do that. That's vertical development, which may seem harder to scale but is nonetheless vital.

The Real-Life Test

Vertical development is not a brand new concept. Various researchers have explored it for years as a means of "expanding your mindset," as one *Forbes* columnist put it. "Your mindset refers to the mental models you engage when you are thinking, as well as your sense of identity. Vertical development isn't about training a leader in skills; it's about transforming the ways a leader thinks, which will impact what they do and how they behave. In vertical development, you pay attention to becoming more adaptable, more self-aware, more collaborative and able to span boundaries and networks."[1]

Vertical development is about transforming the ways a leader thinks, which will impact what they do and how they behave.

That's a good big-picture summary. But I have, over time, developed a particular version of the practice. When I first encountered vertical development as an idea, it made intuitive sense to me: My direct experience training and coaching had taught me that linear, "horizontal" approaches that involved acquiring a prefab set of skills weren't squaring with the real dilemmas leaders faced. There was a distinct need to help them build that capacity to face uncertainty and deploy skills situationally.

And yet, the versions of vertical development I first encountered were presented as a step-by-step, one-size-fits-all program: First you do this, second you do that, and so on until you've checked all the boxes in the right order. That struck me as a very horizontal methodology—a static set of prefab stages. It treated vertical development as, essentially, a different batch of skills to acquire.

Again, skill acquisition is important, at all levels of an organization. Early in my career, before I turned to coaching, I was a trainer specializing in so-called soft skills: communication skills, leadership skills, and so on. We used role-playing and other methods, and the training was perfectly effective. But I found that the participants in those sessions always wanted to know the same thing: "Yeah, this is really good," they'd say, "but how do I actually use this when I go back to the office?"

After our training sessions, we would do a sort of debriefing in three parts, which we called "Head, Heart, Home." Head meant, Did you understand the exercise? Do you see what the methodology is?

Heart referred to how the skill or practice or behavior felt—how it felt to do it, the impact on the other party, the participants' comfort with the skill. Those two discussions were pretty straightforward.

But Home was the big one: How will you actually use this? And that would end up taking a long, long time. People would understand the training and see the value. But when they tried to think about how it would play out in practice, they had lots of questions: *How would I use it in this situation? What about with this kind of person? What if the person is more senior than me? Do I use it in this situation? How do I use it in another situation? What does this look like when I'm actually in a conversation with my manager or my disgruntled employee or somebody else?*

They wanted to know when—and how—to apply which skill in real life.

And they were absolutely right to want that, because if a person didn't get the application nailed down, the skill would just fall off or fade away. So I spent more and more time focused on what is commonly called "transfer of learning"—instilling confidence not only in a particular skill but in being able to actually use that skill in real-life workplace scenarios.

In a sense, it's that real-life test that led me to coaching—the realization that you can't solve a vertical problem with ever-more-horizontal development. And these days, organizations face more vertical problems. Generic solutions don't help with a workforce that's increasingly diverse, in terms of gender, ethnicity, and generations. The pandemic only accelerated a splintering of longstanding workplace norms, from expectations around remote work to career ambitions. Add to that economic and technological uncertainty. Competition is fierce: What if the product we're working on is made obsolete by some new development tomorrow? Every day is an adventure.

You can't solve a vertical problem with ever-more-horizontal development.

Having all the right skills is of little use if you can't apply them, appropriately and helpfully.

But again: that's real life. So how do you deal with it? Just adding skills isn't enough. Skills are crucial, but they are only the beginning. Having all the right skills is of little use if you can't apply them, appropriately and helpfully.

That's Not a Nail

Vertical development responds to a contemporary workplace that is not just unpredictable but diverse and complex in ways that would have been unthinkable to past generations. It's focused on developing judgment about what skill to apply in what situation to try to gain an appropriate outcome. One of the core lessons of vertical development is that to be successful, you have to be alert, aware, and present around what's happening in the moment. If you aren't—if, instead, you're just dialing in past behavioral patterns—you can't properly judge what skill to apply and how.

Maybe you've heard another of the old saws I grew up with as a kid in the South: If your only tool is a hammer, then everything looks like a nail. The same applies here. If you just have a small set of skills, you're going to apply them regardless. And sometimes they're going to work and sometimes they're not.

But a much more advanced and sophisticated approach starts with seeing the problem for what it really is—not as a reflection of what's handy in your tool kit.

Vertical development is also about how to do that without getting super stressed or reactive. In other words, being able to deal with a volatile environment, and being able to respond, not just react.

In the martial arts, you train to learn a set of skills—and everyone learns the same skills. What matters is the application of those skills. The difference between a good martial artist and a so-so one isn't really skill mastery. It's being able to remain present and apply the appropriate skill at the appropriate time in the appropriate way.

For example, if you have developed the ability to really injure somebody, and you apply that to a person who looked at you funny, well, that wasn't an appropriate application of that skill. If somebody has a gun to your head, that may be the appropriate time to break out that dangerous skill application! But to be able to tell the difference between the stink-eye and a gun—that requires presence and self-awareness. The repeated incidents in the news of events like this show that it is not as easy and obvious as it sounds.

Our human brains are very habituated. If you are not present to what's happening in the moment, you are likely to just go back to your patterns. Being present lets you see how things are right now, not how they have usually been in the past. Only then are you able to make an assessment of what needs to happen, a proper judgment of what skills to apply, what approach to take, all based on what's current, not familiar.

Particularly when people are stressed, they make bad decisions precisely because everything unexpected feels like a threat. Or, you could say, everything looks like a nail—even when it's actually a fresh shoot, a fragile new stalk that should be cultivated and encouraged to grow. And if you can't see that, it doesn't matter how good your hammering skills may be.

Interweaving

While I'm often surprised at how much of the traditional corporate world still finds these ideas novel and difficult to fully understand, I do cross paths with kindred spirits. One is Carlo Bos, co-CEO for the Co-Active Training Institute, who has a couple of decades of experience with leadership development and has seen the same revolution that I see. In one of our exchanges, he brought forth some insights that might help make it clear how horizontal and vertical development complement each other—how they are, and in fact must be, interwoven.[2]

Specifically, he made a distinction between development from the outside-in, and the inside-out. Horizontal development—the acquisition of skills, knowledge, information—is essentially "an outside-in move," as Carlo put it. "It's 'how I get things done in my job.'" I think of this as filling a person's cup. The learning, skill, and knowledge are poured into the individual from the outside. Vertical development, meanwhile, is an inside-out process, focused on leaders expanding their ability to engage and respond to diverse business conditions. "It's enabling an internal capacity to develop, take on, incorporate new points of view and perspectives and the capacity to observe, to engage in those situations uniquely."

And here's the point he made that may be most important: "There's a relationship that's ongoing between the outside-in learning and the inside-out learning. Because as I take on new skills, it informs who I am and how I respond as a leader. That learning can change me, which changes how I use the skill."

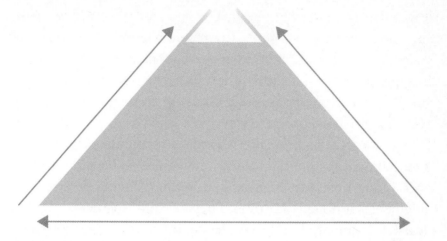

FIGURE 6.4 Horizontal and vertical development work together.

This idea of interweaving the horizontal and vertical is really important to underscore (Figure 6.4). We're not talking about having horizontal and vertical stand side by side. We're actually talking about each informing the other. And as much as that's a challenge, it's also potentially exciting. To borrow from Carlo one last time: A leader or potential leader has to be willing to grow, but if they are, then they will find vertical development encourages growth. And as a leader or potential leader grows, "so does their capacity and effectiveness in leading in more complexity."

Ultimately this gets to what has historically been one of the more intangible elements of effective leadership—something that's been almost an "It" factor. Certain leaders just have "It"— and you just know it when you see it. Really, though, "It" isn't that mysterious, but is rather precisely that ability to deal with complexity with a mix of skill and judgment.

Employees who are looking to advance in the leadership ranks are sometimes confused about this, because organizations focus so much on step-by-step horizontal development that it leaves them wondering: "Wait, I've acquired all the skills, why am I not getting promoted?" Right now there's not even a language to talk about what's missing—that "It" factor, the capacity to apply the right skills the right way, at the right time. How do you help these potential leaders develop so they can progress? How do you more concretely evaluate who has those capacities? I do think that traditional corporate environments knew this. The standard in the mid- to late 1900s was to develop leaders over a long time, say 20 years. They knew the development of judgment was honed over time. They may not have called it "vertical development," but they understood that this was required to be an exceptional leader. Now the time horizon for this type of leader development is greatly reduced. Most leaders no longer stay at one company for 20-plus years. It is difficult to cultivate the needed level of expertise, judgment, and self-awareness in fits and starts at multiple different companies. There has to be a new way of tracking vertical leader development for an individual across multiple companies to have the same (or better) impact as in the past when employees stayed at one company for their entire career.

Maximum Capacities

One challenge around vertical development is finding a way to measure it—to quantify the return on investment. It's a concept that's built around the belief that you need something more than an industrial-era skill checklist. And as much as organizations now recognize the need for a more nuanced and flexible approach, everybody still wants a checklist. It's a conundrum.

And it's understandable. So I'll say more in chapters ahead, especially in this book's final section, about how vertical

Table 6.1 Twenty-first-century leader development

Skills	Capabilities	Capacity
Develop new competencies, processes, tools, or models that help leaders deliver on their tactical role expectations more effectively.	Develop combined sets of skills and mindsets used to impact the daily business of the organization more strategically as a leader.	Develop a leader's ability to contain, manage, or affect change in the evolving set of circumstances within their role.

development might be measured and tracked. But first I want to say a little more about what it is; I'll start with the big picture, then share a few specific examples.

From the highest level, vertical development is about leadership *growth*. And, maybe more to the point, about cultivating the self-awareness that leadership growth requires.

What does that mean? It means an awareness and ability to comprehend one's own thinking, sensing, emotional effectiveness, and ability to comprehend and engage with different types of circumstances or variables. It means developing more (and more) *capacity* to deal with more (and more) complexity.

It means developing more (and more) capacity to deal with more (and more) complexity.

It might be helpful to identify a kind of bridge between *skill* and *capacity* (Table 6.1). We'll go deeper on this in the book's final section, but at Sounding Board we have identified an interim term between "skill" and "capacity" that's useful to understand. We use the word "capabilities" to refer to the ability to combine multiple skills and to use those skills in an interconnected way. So, for example, combine the skill of critical thinking with the skill of breaking problems down to understandable pieces, and you can call that the capability of strategic thinking. (For more specific examples of capabilities, see the box at the end of this chapter.)

From there, you can break down that idea of the broader capacity to deal with complexity into a set of more specific capacities: flexibility, pattern recognition, and self-regulation. In each category, there are emotional, cognitive, motivational, and behavioral variations.

For example: Cognitive flexibility means a capacity for awareness. The emotional variation of pattern recognition entails developing empathy. Behavioral self-regulation reflects a capacity for focus. At the next level down, these translate to capabilities like interpersonal skills, strategic thinking, being able to set a vision and direction, conflict management, cooperative problem solving, and more.

I'll break this down further—and describe some pioneering attempts to measure development outcomes tied to these goals—in the book's final section. For now I'll offer a couple of concrete examples of how vertical development matters in real-world situations, right now.

The Right Timing

Not long ago, a founder and CEO client of mine was blindsided when told that his board of directors wanted him out, and that he should come up with a transition plan. As you might imagine, he had a pretty emotional reaction. And, of course, in such situations, that emotional reaction typically leaves people able to think of just two options.

One, basically, is: Screw you, I quit.

And the other: Screw you, I am not leaving.

That's usually as far as the reactionary thinking goes. It's binary, flight or flight. But as we've seen, this is a moment to step back. What do you really want? What's the larger context, and how does this one decision fit into that context? What's the right move right now?

I've seen scenarios like this plenty of times. Sometimes it's better to fight to stay on, sometimes it's a perfect opportunity to move on. And that's the point. There's no single right answer or easy checklist that works for everyone. Finding your way to the right answer depends on exactly what vertical development is meant to address: evaluating the context, and timing.

This isn't just a CEO problem. Leaders from the C-suite to supervisor face these crossroad decisions, and no amount of horizontal training alone can resolve them.

My blindsided CEO client had plenty of skills or he wouldn't have gotten to such a successful place in his career in the first place. That wasn't the question. The question was: given what you want, what are your options for managing this situation? And what kinds of approaches and skills can you use to manage the outcome?

Vertical development helps frame the answers to those questions. A coach, in this situation, becomes the "thinking partner" I described earlier—not someone who announces what to do based on some prescribed checklist, but, rather, someone who helps the leader-at-a-crossroads see beyond a short-term binary choice. *Here are five ways you might manage this; which seems to be the best?* The answer will usually be a little bit of this and a little bit of that—and it will *always* come from the leader themselves. After all, it is their decision.

One key element in this thought-partner discussion is timing. Yes, you have the skill to take a certain approach, but when is the right time to apply that approach? Sometimes thinking through timing can be *the* critical factor. In the scenario of the CEO being threatened by the board, the right course might be: "I'm gonna stay for six months, and I have a plan to increase revenue by 50% (or whatever); if you still think it's not working after six months, then we'll transition." This is what another one of my clients did that I described earlier—and it worked. After six months, the board's attitude shifted to "Please stay; you can't leave!"

Clearly that's always a much better plan than just a hot-reaction "screw you." And this CEO client ended up crafting a transition plan that satisfied his board—and him. But what's really interesting isn't the details of that specific outcome. It's that, in my experience, when a leader at a crossroads steps back and thinks about timing and context, and comes up with a plan for managing what happens next, then whichever path they choose, they can almost always make it happen. The ones who wanted to stay and came up with a plan for that were able to stay. The ones who didn't, came up with a plan for that and were able to go on their own terms.

Context Is King

Mastering timing is a particularly salient and relatable example of why vertical development is so vital. In contrast, mastering *context* may be a notably wide-ranging one—and maybe the trickiest. But here's a clear, specific manifestation of what it means to master context.

In recent years, "listening" has emerged as a key skill. At one point, something like 80% of the CEOs said listening was the number-one skill they were looking for in their leaders. That's a horizontal issue: You can train listening skills. Many did, and no doubt that had positive effects.

Still, listening skills don't magically make everyone a better leader. Often what would happen is, a leader would listen to their team, their employees, their colleagues, whoever. Then the meeting would be over . . . and nothing would happen.

So after some period of time the leader would want to know: "Hey, I'm listening. Why isn't this working? Why isn't anything really changing, progressing?"

The answer is that listening is just one skill. And because of the complexity of the actual workplace, vertical development requires being able to apply multiple skill sets at the appropriate time and in the appropriate context. If you're listening when somebody's really having a big problem, but they don't want advice, they just want to talk it out—that's fine. But if you're listening to the manager in a meeting that needs to lead to a decision, and no one makes a decision—that's not good.

Breakthrough

Now I need to take a step back. I know firsthand that when an actual leader is faced with an actual unanticipated dilemma—whether it's a showdown with the board or something less dramatic—they don't care about all the thought and research around vertical versus horizontal development. Their mode is more primal: "I have this problem. What should I do?"

It starts earlier, building the capacity to deal with the unexpected before the unexpected arrives.

Vertical development responds to that question in a couple of ways. I've described how a good coach can help serve as a real-time thinking partner, helping a leader consider options beyond the gut reaction binary choices. But the real value is deeper than that. It starts earlier, building the capacity to deal with the unexpected before the unexpected arrives.

Finding help building that capacity is surprisingly rare, especially compared to all the horizontal training that's available.

There are innumerable online classes and training programs to teach every skill you can think of. But that's not preparing future leaders for this volatile, unpredictable environment, which is all about deciding how and when to use which skills and capabilities. That's what vertical development can do.

Vertical development is about confronting uncertainty head-on—and that's why people resist the idea at first, but ultimately concede its necessity. Everyone prefers certainty to uncertainty. But the twenty-first century has taught us all that "certainty" is a dangerous desire. Because it's seldom "certain."

For all the steep challenges of contemporary work culture in the past few years, one of the silver linings is that all the change and uncertainty has caused people to start to revive their relationship with themselves. You could say, in fact, that vertical development is about the concept of a leader, or aspiring leader, being in better relationship with themselves. And as a business owner and leader myself, I want to have employees who are in relationship with themselves and want to be working in my business. It's good for an organization's culture, productivity, innovation, creativity, collaboration.

Measuring all of that in a way that's easy to digest is an ongoing project, but in the real world I see this epiphany happen with clients all the time. They realize that just having the skills isn't enough. It's true from the top down into the aspiring ranks: *I took a class on negotiation, and I still got killed in that negotiation with the business partner or on my salary. Why?* Because skills are not enough. Skills are only step one. Organizations obsess about them because they're very tangible and easily measured: Did I get the skill or not? It's harder to measure the application of skills. But that's what really matters, and when leaders figure that out, it's truly the breakthrough point.

Coach: You're close to a breakthrough; here are some ideas for how to make it happen.

1. Remove your mental obstacles. What is the story you are telling yourself that is stopping you from breaking through?

2. Take the risk! Push yourself forward. It is easy to fall back to what is familiar.

3. Remember to reassess what you want. This might change during the breakdown.

4. Let yourself be surprised. Once you break through, things will feel and look different.

5. Be nice to yourself. Forgive yourself for not breaking through yet. This is hard!

6. Look for signs. Notice when you do break through. It can be subtle, dramatic, or disconcerting.

Coach: Which of these will help you move forward?

The Third Right Answer

> *The way I see it, I've got two choices. I need your help deciding.*
>
> **Coach: Actually, you need help seeing that there are more than two choices.**
>
> *Wait, how do you know?*
>
> **Coach: Because there are always more choices!**

Rethinking—and updating—your approach to leadership might at times sound exhausting. And let's face it, sometimes it can be. But along the way, there are many payoffs, many moments when you can breathe a sigh of relief, because you've built the skills and capacity to handle an unexpected crisis. You've put in the time and energy to learn how to confront difficult challenges.

I've found this with many coaching clients: At a certain point in a coaching cycle, the sessions can get shorter because the coachee, based on what they've learned, is anxious to take action. By this time the trust in the coach–coachee relationship is deeply established; each understands how the other works. Together they've essentially developed a kind of shorthand for their conversations—almost a private language that serves just them.

The work of the coaching is . . . mutually thinking about options and knowing there is not one right answer.

This is when you know a thinking partnership is fully established. The work of the coaching is now not so much the coach driving the development forward as it is mutually thinking about options and knowing there is not one right answer.

It's liberating, and refreshing. But even a true breakthrough doesn't mean the coaching is over. In fact, it's really just a another new starting point. I'll give you an example.

When I have worked with new CEOs, I have often had to help them stop clinging to their previous role, or the roles of other deputies, and get them to fully take on the CEO role. The underlying challenge is familiar: Being CEO was new and unknown, so they veered back toward doing what they were used to, and knew they excelled at. Figuring out their new responsibilities seemed like an unimaginable task.

Working through this process can take months (taking the steps I've been describing, letting go of the past, figuring out true wants and goals, and so on). In the case of new CEOs I could always tell they'd had a breakthrough when they would say either "I don't have anything to do" or "I don't know what to do." This meant they had finally let go of doing every *other* job but the CEO job they actually held. And now they were ready to take that on—but they needed to figure out what that meant. There's some version of this in every good coaching engagement. That's why a breakthrough can be a new beginning.

Everything up to now has been preliminary. It means that now the coachee can really begin to do the work that matters. At the CEO level or any other level, they've broken through to a new way of thinking and operating. It can be scary because it means standing on ground they have never stood on before. It's a new perspective that makes everything look very different.

How Do I Think about This?

The natural arc of a coaching engagement begins with a broad focus. As you engage, each session tends to get more and more specific, until it becomes about one thing that you're trying to get through to the other side of. It's about one specific place to apply the learning. To explain, I'll tell you a quick story that will illuminate how that plays out.

I had a particular CEO client I coached for quite a long time. In the beginning, it took a lot of time for him to understand what we were doing. But after a while we knew each other so well, and we got so good with our process, that our calls would go like this:

"Hi, Lori. Here's the thing I'm thinking about." And he would take maybe five minutes to sketch whatever that situation was. And then he would say: "Frame it for me." Or, better yet, "Reframe it for me."

I'd take it in and think about it for a bit, then I'd offer at least three ways he might proceed: "You could think about this way, that way, or this other way." Each scenario was reasonable and rational—the point wasn't to guide him to one answer, it was to offer three scenarios that struck me as perfectly legitimate, based on what he'd told me and what I knew.

And then we'd go a little bit through each of those three frames, and talk about how it might play out. As we did this, the process would always lead him to say, "Okay, it's this one." Or it might be, in effect, a fourth option—"it's this one, but with a twist that this discussion made me think of just now." As soon as it clicked for him, he was ready to go.

What he needed help with, in other words, wasn't "What should I do?" It was "How do I think about this?"

You'll notice, I hope, that this stands in contrast with the typical belief that, whatever this CEO's situation was, there was just *one* right answer out there, and the goal was to find someone to tell him what that was. World-class athletes have a coach, not a consultant. Sure, they might have specialty consultants like a nutritionist, for example, but they can't get to this level of performance and stay there without a coach. At this level of performance, the coach is not working with the athlete on skill development. It is all about the awareness and judgment needed to apply the skills they have in the most exceptional way in the most critical moment.

So more broadly, the goal isn't to find someone who will tell you, "Here is your answer." It's to see that "You can think about it like this, this, this, or possibly this." And you can proceed from that to determine the right course, with the right timing, given a proper understanding of the full context.

Beyond Binary

For some, this can be a challenge. Many of us have become wired to narrow everything down to binary-choice decision making: everything gets reduced to yes or no, stay or go, A or B. And we don't even realize this is how we're thinking.[1]

I had one client who swore he was not a binary thinker, and had a whole story about his science-grounded background to demonstrate why this was so. Then, he proceeded to tell me that each day, driving home, he assessed for himself whether his day had been good or bad.

I pointed out that this was a classic example of binary framing that actually *limits* your thinking. His days were so complex, this evaluation couldn't be accurate, let alone useful. He was shocked but admitted that somehow it made him "feel better" if he could say more days were good than bad. Maybe so, but it wasn't helping him honestly assess what was going on, and therefore wouldn't help him make decisions in the future.

I started pointing out to him every time he brought up an either/or choice. He didn't realize how often that's what he was doing. "Okay, that's your A and B," I'd say. "What's C and D?"

He was a very experienced CEO, and really was accomplished as a leader and a scientist. But this habit had started to cause problems. In addition to limiting his options, this approach often came across to his team as ultimatums.

And even after he acknowledged the issue, it took months to get him out of the habit. That required cultivating a new habit of considering alternate frames of reference and alternate solutions, every time. Eventually, the potentially better outcomes became more visible to him; he could create alternate options himself. This forced him to get clear on what he wanted each time.

Getting past binary thinking was key to that change. Taking a binary thinking approach can be a way to avoid achieving clarity about what you want, because what you want is often not available in the A-or-B format. And when you feel that's the case, why waste the time thinking about anything other than A or B? Not surprisingly, this limits innovation and creativity.

There are a few reasons that the post-binary approach is so effective. One is that binary decision-making—you can do A or you can do B—is often not just limiting, but false. If you only have A or B, you're squeezed. And because it's implied that these are the *only* options, your thinking and creativity are limited.

Years ago I came across a really useful idea related to this from Roger von Oech, a creativity expert who wrote a book called *A Whack on the Side of the Head*. He had a set of cards called the "creative whack pack," and each card prompted you to think more creatively. There were dozens of them, but one stuck with me because it rang so true. It said: "Look for the third right answer." So I always try to offer a minimum of three options—and I want each of them to be potentially "right."

The first answer is often the one you've already been doing, or is the common, "obvious" answer that most everyone else would choose. The second one is almost always the easy one. It's not wrong, it's just not very challenging. It's safe. You have to think through both of those before you can properly consider a more creative one, which is rarely top of mind. Something that's not easy or obvious or familiar. But it's not wrong. It's the third right answer.

Again, the first two are not wrong either. The first one you've already been basically doing. It's your habitual approach. But the whole point of coaching is to go beyond your habitual approach, because this is what is going to help you reach your potential.

And then there's the second option, the easiest one, the one that somebody else told you to do, or that, in the age of social media, is almost always the one that "everybody" seems to be doing—that's the typical default answer.

Often, those are your binary choices, your A or B.

But to get something innovative, interesting, creative, new, you usually have to go, at a minimum, to choice number three.

> *To get something innovative, interesting, creative, new, you usually have to go, at a minimum, to choice number three.*

Embrace the Unexpected

One element of the practice of Tai Chi involves training yourself to perform and execute certain movements over and over again. The goal is to make each movement so familiar you're not conscious of it in the moment of application: Once the movement is initiated, your body memory just kicks in and starts doing it. This creates a sense of being relaxed in the moment because you do not actually have to *think* about it. Your body knows what to do without conscious mental effort. This is necessary in a martial arts scenario because thinking can take too long. We have a saying: "The T in thinking is too slow." In other words, by the time your mind gets to "T," the opponent has already knocked you over.

But actually, the goal is more than that. Because you aren't just learning one movement; you're learning many. And the real goal is to know them *all* so well that, if you begin one movement in response to

> *This dynamic ability to cycle through a variety of options echoes the practice of finding a third (or fourth or fifth) right answer.*

a particular pattern, and that pattern unexpectedly changes, you can naturally adjust. Without stopping and thinking about it, you seamlessly transition to a different, appropriate movement.

After all, in an actual sparring match, it will rarely be a simple matter of *I push you; you fall over*. It's more like I push you—and you move. I push you in a different way—you move again. But I learn each time, and try a different push—this time you're unbalanced and step out. It's this dynamic movement, the ability to cycle through a variety of options, each executed naturally, that echoes the practice of finding a third (or fourth or fifth) right answer. After some practice, the player can see beyond the first couple of moves to know what the opponent is going to do, almost before they know themselves. Their binary responses are visible and obvious, and the experienced player can easily move past those to the response that gets the impact they want.

Tai Chi is *really* all about getting to that place where you're going beyond your regular rote patterns—beyond fight or flight. If you're doing your rote pattern, your sparring partner already knows what you're going to do. So they're already responding before you even finish your pattern. So, yes, sometimes the first move works; you wouldn't have made it if you didn't believe it could. But often it's a follow-up move, one that nobody (even you!) expected that actually does the trick.

When that happens in Tai Chi, the two people sparring sometimes actually end up laughing. Because the resolution was so unexpected, both sides are surprised: "What just happened?" we ask, chuckling together.

This gets at what can be so special about the third right answer—it can be delightful in a way that was impossible to anticipate when you started the process of tackling whatever the problem or challenge might have been.

There are a couple of key points here. One is that, as in Tai Chi, you can't arrive at that surprising solution if you haven't built up your repertoire of fully mastered skills. When you're in the middle of sparring, there's no time to stop and think about what new push might be handy here. It's happening in the moment. If you are trying to think about it, then by the time you've thought through the whole situation, the moment has already passed. (At that point, in fact, chances are good that *you've* been pushed out of the ring.)

Something similar is going on with a leader confronting a real-world challenge, although generally you have more thinking time than a few seconds. You might try the first and the second solution, and those don't give you the result you want. But a complex environment basically requires you to keep trying to find that third right answer—something that would never have occurred to you at the outset.

A complex environment requires you to keep trying to find that third right answer— something that would never have occurred to you at the outset.

As in Tai Chi there is no simple formula for arriving at that new choice. Often it comes through collaboration with others who may see the problem or issue with a different lens—which of course is precisely the role a coach can play.

More specifically, opening new options comes from continually asking (or thinking):

- "How can we reframe this?"
- "What's another way to think about this?"
- "What possible options haven't we considered yet?"
- "What's the most unexpected thing we could do here?"
- Even something as straightforward: "What if A and B don't work?"

These are all great coaching questions, and anyone can use them.

Another client of mine had this kind of expansive thinking in spades. He would always ask, "What is plan C?" And when that answer was clear, he would ask "Okay, What about plan D?" I saw him get to plan F on a regular basis. His company was visibly innovative. Everyone there knew bringing an A or B choice wasn't going to be enough.

And that's the second key point: Often the unexpected nature of that outcome is not just surprising, but *delightfully* surprising.

The word "delight" gets tossed around a lot (especially by tech companies), but I don't use it lightly. What is delightful is when something happens that meets your need in a way that you didn't anticipate, let alone expect. That's the delightful part. As in Tai Chi, there's a little bit of magic in the unexpected successful outcome of the third right answer.

> *There's a little bit of magic in the unexpected successful outcome of the third right answer.*

The unexpected answer is, ultimately, the place of innovation. That's the place of going beyond what you normally do, or what everyone does. That's delight.

An example of this delight happened just as I was writing this chapter. An employee sent me this message in response to some plans for next year that we just announced, and that offered some surprises. (Actually, this specifically concerned a new approach to performance reviews that I'll describe in this book's final section. In a nutshell, we didn't choose to continue reviews as usual [option A] or junk the process altogether [option B], but, rather, to arrive at a new approach altogether.) "So amazing! I always appreciate how intentional you are at breaking the mold here about 'what other companies do' and creating the type of company culture that you know/believe will care for your employees!! Thank you isn't enough!!"

This shows the impact of the delight that comes from unexpected solutions to problems. (And it's incredibly gratifying for the leader, too.)

I experienced another example of this some years ago when I was out of town, rented a car and received a Ford Mustang. After a long day of meetings and an evening event, I went to the parking garage and it was dark. I barely remembered what car I had rented and certainly didn't remember where I had parked it and couldn't see anything in the dim light. I pressed the key fob, hoping to hear the beeping of the car unlocking. Instead, a lighted picture of a mustang shined on the floor. I was delighted. Not only could I find my car, the picture reminded me what car I had rented; it was such a surprise that I gasped.

Judgment

Thinking of the third right answer doesn't mean doing crazy things, or just doing something a different way to be rebellious or unconventional. Change has an impact that can be good—or not. So what's required is a measure of judgment. Recognizing a range of options is just the (necessary) first step toward superior judgment.

Recognizing a range of options is just the (necessary) first step toward superior judgment.

This judgment isn't just a matter of a single decision point. It's something that's required of leaders throughout all their decisions, conversations, and actions. The most innovative, creative solution still has to work in the leader's specific context. It still has to be communicated and rolled out successfully. It still needs a thoughtful assessment of potential consequences as well as payoffs.

Often, judgment comes from experience—a feeling of what works absorbed from the many failures and wins over time. It can also be developed through focused observation and pattern recognition. It requires the ability to recognize your own emotions and biases and weed them out of the decision-making process. The deep knowledge of the context combined with this experience blend to develop a sense of judgment that can be utilized to make decisions quickly even in volatile or unknown circumstances.

The judgment of what works when trying novel approaches is honed over time. More seasoned leaders have better judgment. Call it "gut feel," intuition, or just the accumulation of experience, this ability is required for the implementation of answers outside the norm. In other words, judgment isn't an easily trainable "skill" in the horizontal development sense, and it's more than the combined-skill capability that I described in Chapter 6. But that said, judgment is a capacity that can be enhanced and developed, and is a critical component of leadership success.

I was lucky because my judgment was honed through my coaching clients. I heard so many stories of what worked and didn't in so many environments that it is as if I worked at 100 different companies. Because I was a neutral outside party, I also had limited biases and could point out the emotions and biases to my coaching clients. That's part of what can make a coach such a helpful thinking partner.

Endless Alternatives

Now just to be clear, I would never simply tell a client: "Frame it this way." When I say there is no single right answer, I mean it.

For starters, someone who is leading a company has financial responsibility, both to investors and to employees, and I am not part of that company. Something similar holds true for leaders of divisions or teams—and it would be very both arrogant and inappropriate of me or any other coach to tell them how to think.

They are the people who are getting paid the big bucks to do that job. Even if they *want* someone to tell them what to do, I can't. And no coach or trainer or development expert should.

What I *can* do is give them some alternatives to open up their minds. And after I explain those preliminary alternatives, my next question is some version of: "Which one do you think is going to work best for you or your circumstances?" "Which one resonates?" "Which is the best fit?" "What other options do you see now?"

In the spirit of the thinking partner idea, this is a very collaborative process. The conversations these questions spark are always shaped around the coachee making a decision. Again, it's their company or job or career, not mine. The coach's job is to help the leader reach a conclusion, not to tell that person what the conclusion should be.

The answer may in fact turn out to be a mix of those scenarios—or some other alternative that the scenarios spark. I am not telling them to think like me, because I'm not the one running that company, or managing that team, or angling to improve that division's results. They're doing that, and I'm giving them alternatives. It's their job to choose; they have the agency and responsibility to make the decision.

I actually drill this into our coaches at my company, because so many coaches out there just want to tell the client how they should think. But they have no clue most of the time what that person's job and role really are. As a coach, you don't want to tell them how to think; you want to help them think. You want to be their thinking partner.

As a coach, you don't want to tell them how to think; you want to help them think. You want to be their thinking partner.

And this is particularly useful as you get deeper into the relationship. The "thinking partner" approach I described earlier can be applied to many situations, and builds on itself. In the case of leadership coaching, you are giving options for how to enhance a leadership capability in this circumstance that then can be applied to many other circumstances. Later, if (or, more likely, when) that leader or aspiring leader hits another problem in the same vein, they have a process for getting through it.

As time goes on, the coach is not just helping solve one specific problem—though that's often what manifests itself—they are modeling a way of problem solving, a method of nonbinary thinking. They are helping the leader develop judgment, and that is a capacity that takes a leader from good to great.

Coach: Seems like you could use some help shifting to a nonbinary thinking approach. Here are some ways to do that.

1. Pay attention to when you are thinking in a binary way. Terms like good/bad and right/wrong are a clue. Avoid framing options/solutions as either/or.

2. Acknowledge that there are always more than two options.

3. Embrace complexity. Binary thinking oversimplifies.

4. Allow yourself to "not know." Not knowing *the* answer gives you space to consider multiple answers.

5. Remember all those multiple-choice test questions in school? Their real purpose was to develop critical thinking. Use your critical thinking skills to get past this bias.

6. Take apart the complexity into multiple pieces. Look for an additive solution that handles the various parts.

7. Avoid yes/no questions and answers. The famous improv game called "Yes, and . . ." can be great for this purpose: Answer "yes," then add to the answer and see where it takes you. Look for multiple options, perspectives, and solutions. Push to have a minimum of three options on the table. If there are only two, ask for more.

Coach: Which of these suggestions might be most impactful for you?

Making New Choices

> *I've had a real breakthrough in my thinking, but I'm confused about my next move.*
>
> **Coach: What's the issue?**
>
> *I keep seeing different options, different angles, different possibilities.*
>
> **Coach: That's a good sign—now it's time to make real decisions.**

You can never be sure exactly when it will happen or what precisely will trigger it, but at some point in a coaching engagement, there's a transition that can feel confusing. It's after that breakthrough period, when the coachee's mind has opened up, and they're truly thinking about things differently. Their eyes are wide open and the third way—and fourth way, and fifth way—start to come more easily.

And now they're suddenly asking a new question: *"What about . . . ?"*

Actually, they can't stop. It's a series of questions. What about this option? What about that other idea? What about how it would work in a different situation?

And they're all good questions! The problem is that the coachee has opened up so much that they're not completely sure how to proceed—whether rethinking an ongoing effort or reacting to an unexpected challenge. It's crucial to build that ability to consider fresh perspectives and let go of the same old solutions. But it's even more crucial to figure out how to act—how to make it real.

I always think this point is the place for courage. It's risky to move beyond conventional thinking. Yet it's exactly when you're not quite sure which answer is the right answer—but you must decide—that you're most likely to discover a "right" choice that you never would have come up with before. It feels so much easier when there is only one choice or a standard choice. There's no room for uncertainty but also no room for innovation.

Learning to frame dilemmas in different ways can open up your choices. *Making* choices depends on understanding your specific context. To spell that out in more detail, let's use some beyond-binary thinking to address a real, specific and very knotty workplace challenge as an example (especially these days): How to foster a sense of connection.

> *Learning to frame dilemmas in different ways can open up your choices.* Making *choices depends on understanding your specific context.*

Community, Not Family

Some organizations, of course, hardly bother to do this at all. Focused exclusively on "the bottom line," they treat employees like interchangeable robots, and offer no clear path to advancement or improvement, let alone any connection to a common purpose. Probably all of us have had at least some experience with such an environment—and eventually quit. This all-business approach is not only borderline inhumane, it's not even good for business. Still, it's sadly commonplace.

In contrast—maybe even in response—many organizations and leaders now emphasize the idea of creating a sense of "belonging," often explicitly linked to the idea of a workplace "family." In fact, some have added belonging to the list of fundamental workplace goals: diversity, equity, inclusion, belonging. Start-ups in particular are prone to this; I know of at least one that actually called its regular all-hands meetings "Fam," short for family.

Sounds good, right? But this approach can be symptomatic of misguided thinking that can turn into a real problem. It's one that can tie directly back to the *in loco parentis*—"in place of parents"—mentality that I described in Chapter 3: thinking of employees practically as children who need to be overseen and cared for over the entirety of their career. Extending that idea, a sense of "belonging" is a psychological construct offering a feeling of safety that is more properly associated with *actual* family. This may have worked when companies were operating "*in loco parentis*" but it is not a current workplace construct that is functional when the average length of employee tenure is so much shorter than in the past. (That start-up learned as much when a business downturn led to layoffs—which were announced at "Fam.")

That's why the attempt to position work as a source of family-level belonging is a mistake. Belonging is a second option for the workplace. How about a third? What I think an organization or leader *can* do is cultivate a sense of community. There's a big difference between belonging and community, and it becomes clear when you step back and consider the fuller context.

Here's the short version. Overlaying a family dynamic onto the work environment in a black and white way can't work because no company is ever going to be successful creating and maintaining that depth of belonging. That's just not the purpose of the workplace.

In fact, that's how a misguided sense of "belonging" can backfire. One company I worked with tried very hard to create a sense of belonging. They had even held dedicated events where people shared their personal history and explained to their whole team why they are as they are. They had a special slogan they invoked to underscore their family-like unity.

Well, then there was a recession. They didn't make their numbers and they had to lay off 25% of the company. Everyone was outraged. Not just the people who were laid off, but every-one. "What happened to belonging? What happened to unity? What happened to being a family? What happened to our lofty slogan?" The result was a mess; people felt betrayed. All of that sense of family and belonging turned out to be conditional. It depended on the health of the business, and the bottom line—as it always must.

That's why companies are better off not promising a sense of belonging. It implies a kind of internal security that no business can guarantee. I know of another company that uses the term *Ohana*, which is Hawaiian for *family*. A company with tens of thousands of employees is *not* a family—it can't be.

Lumping in *belonging* with diversity, equity, and inclusion is particularly fraught. A company absolutely can, and in this era I'd say must, promise to be unbiased. We can guarantee we're not going to fire or demote or isolate or discriminate you for your race, sexual orientation, age, gender. But unbiased is not the same thing as unconditional.

> *But unbiased is not the same thing as unconditional.*

Community is a realistic framework—and, ultimately, the better answer. Community still involves connectedness, the sense that you have a community of co-workers or community of colleagues. Perhaps even more than that: a community of like-minded thinkers who have similar values in relation to the company. These are things a leader can cultivate, and a work-place can deliver. It's also a clear alternative to the all-business model that ignores the value of connection altogether.

So diversity, equity, inclusion? Yes. Community? Yes. Human-ity? Absolutely yes.

But belonging? No, that is not something the workplace is designed to provide.

What, then, are the characteristics of community that a leader can cultivate and encourage, without falling into the trap of promising something approaching familial belonging?

To start, lean into the fact that it makes intuitive sense that you can and should feel connected to other people who are doing something similar to you. Community, in general, works best when it's built around a common interest. That's how Facebook communities work. I have an interest in a show or a sports team, a hobby or a cause, so I want to talk to other people who have that same interest. I'm a new parent, a fan of contemporary fiction, a gardening enthusiast, or whatever, so I want to connect with others who are, too. Community simply needs a common interest.

That translates intuitively to work. You have a natural starting point or built-in potential for common interest: You all work at the same place. So leadership's contribution can be to articulate and amplify a sense of shared purpose, and to create a culture that feels supportive to employees. If it's a community, you should, for example, be encouraged to ask questions of other people, give ideas to other people, and expect that other people are going to help you out. This is less like a family than a neighborhood.

You have a natural starting point or built-in potential for common interest: You all work at the same place.

But there's another element of community that echoes all this, and it is particularly applicable to the workplace: education. Joining and frequenting a Facebook group devoted to your favorite show may not sound like education, but sharing knowledge and ideas and observations about a common interest is a form of community glue. Leadership can address that directly. When an employee faces a challenge, they should feel there's a community of colleagues to ask advice, help out, and otherwise support them. Ideally, no one is left out from receiving that kind of backup.

Fostering cross-functional interaction, employee resource groups, informal social opportunities, and employee skill sharing are all good approaches to foster the exchange of information and opinion. One approach we use at Sounding Board is to start every large meeting with a "Connection Exercise." This could be a paired discussion, a small group task, an individual reflection, a large group activity, even having employees rate their current sense of well-being. We vary the approach to accommodate different interaction styles and focus on having employees learn from one another.

That's still different from promising a sense of belonging that is more of an individual construct. In a community, one can choose to be part of the community, or one can choose not to be part of the community. Leadership can only do what's in its power to help everyone feel welcome and, hopefully, choose to participate.

But creating a sense of belonging is beyond anything leadership can deliver. A sense of belonging is an individual, internal construct, requiring something like unconditional love. Can a company really deliver that? I don't think so. For starters, both managers and employees are there to perform a job. If the worker isn't performing, the manager is going to have a problem with that. That's a conditional relationship.

Cooperative Competition

I've referred to Tai Chi a few times as a helpful behavioral model, and you might assume that the community that forms around the practice would be an enlightened example of near-familial connection. But in my experience, it's much more complicated than that in ways that are useful to understand.

There's no question that a lot of people who come to the practice try to tap into a sense of belonging in the community around it. And there certainly *is* a community. But the reality is, you're also competing with each other. For starters, you're literally sparring. More than that, Tai Chi doesn't have a "belt" system; instead, you are simply ranked within your community. Somebody is the top, often the most senior student, somebody is second, and so on down to the lowest-ranked novices. It's quite cut-and-dried. We're never all at the same level. Everyone is always ranked.

Not surprisingly, this leads to competitiveness, which, in the Tai Chi community I joined and became a part of, created some conflict with the whole "belonging" idea.

A Tai Chi school may seem very far removed from the twenty-first-century workplace, but the issues were surprisingly analogous. Some participants were bringing the wrong set of expectations. They were bringing family-like expectations to something that was not a family. In this case, it could be even more confusing because of some of the language used in some Tai Chi schools, emphasizing your "elders," your "older brother," and so on in a distinctly familial way.

But inside all that, ultimately, was competition. When things got too competitive, people's sense of belonging got knocked off-balance (physically and emotionally). Then, if there was too much emphasis on the belonging side, people didn't compete well, because they didn't want to undermine that family sense by unbalancing others or "winning." They felt badly that their "family member" then had to lose.

So how do you reconcile community and competition? It took quite a while before we landed on the phrase "cooperative competition"—the competition within the school was for everyone's development. Pulling out your most competitive side should happen when competing with people from *other* schools. That blend of connection and competition ended up working out well, creating a really nice community. Everyone raised their level of martial ability from the competitiveness, but it wasn't so brutal that people didn't still feel a connection with each other. It's a concrete example of the "unity of opposites" idea I brought up back in Chapter 1—in this case, unifying cooperation and competitiveness.

Developing this kind of cooperative competition in the workplace starts with the connection. When employees feel connected to each other and the common goal of the company, the environment is ripe for constructive conflict and rigorous intellectual debate. Ideas, approaches, and solutions can be actively discussed, and differing points of view can be raised, debated, and resolved without the personal distractions that so often derail deep discussions at work. In other words, employees can disagree with each other and still know everyone is working toward the same goal.

> *When employees feel connected to each other and the common goal of the company, the environment is ripe for constructive conflict and rigorous intellectual debate.*

The Balanced Equation

I'll give an example of a senior leader I've worked with who confronted the difference. Basically, this person had responsibility for two primary functions, and he felt he couldn't do them both. "This job is killing me," he told his supervisor. "I don't want to do it anymore. I only want to be responsible for one function."

His manager was apparently surprised, but agreed—with some clarifications. Most notably, if his job and responsibilities changed, his salary would reflect that.

This leader was taken off guard: "I thought you wanted me to be happy here!" His supervisor confirmed that the company *did* want him to be happy there. "But we're operating a business and we can't pay you the same amount if you only have half the responsibility." This was borderline traumatic for this person, because he had assumed the company would meet all his needs, in line with his sense of "belonging."

Broadly, I have a concept I call the "balanced equation." In a nutshell, it means that whatever agreement you're having can be thought of as an equation—and needs to have an equal sign in the middle.

In this case, this person was doing a certain amount of work, for (let's say, to make it easy) $100,000. That was the equation, with an equal sign in the middle. Now he wanted to change one side of the equation (less work and responsibility), but wanted the other side to stay the same. That's not balanced anymore.

The whole idea of belonging is what throws this off. This person felt the company should prioritize his needs over those of the company. He wanted an unbalanced equation. Ironically, he had not been promised any familial sense of belonging—he brought that with him, specifically because his prior workplace had been so brutal. Many people come to new jobs with PTSD around their previous workplaces, so they might mistake community-building with some version of family belonging.

But that's especially true if a company actively uses "family"-related language. That's why it's important not to slip into a mode of just being encouraging all the time, but always actually telling the truth, providing clear feedback and keeping the equation properly balanced.

"I thought you cared about me!" this person told his supervisor. "I do," they said. "But that has to be balanced against the needs of the company." After all, someone else would have to be paid to pick up the responsibilities he was dropping. So he was still welcome in the company community under the new circumstances he'd requested. But it was time to revisit the equal sign, and make this a balanced equation again.

The Pandemic Effect

The pandemic had an effect on all this—both for individuals and for organizations.

Being cut off from the office meant that people who had sought a sense of belonging from their jobs were forced to find it outside of work. It turned out that an employer simply couldn't deliver the level of "family" that some workers craved. From the worker's frame of reference, the limitations of workplace belonging suddenly became obvious.

Meanwhile, most companies didn't know how to foster a community virtually; often their sense of community was really just a side effect of proximity. And without proximity, that kind of fell apart.

That's why even companies that promoted the "family" version of belonging were not immune from the Great Resignation that followed the pandemic. Employees saw through the veil: "I went home and never saw my co-workers, and guess what? I didn't have any sense of loss. I actually had a sense of relief. That whole 'family' thing was BS."

What that means for organizations now is that leaders need to understand and acknowledge the difference between community and family. But that's not all. They also have to be communicative and consistent. Once again, what really matters aren't just the specific leadership skills or even capabilities necessary to build community; it's the ability to observe and understand the broader context, expand the capacity of leaders and proceed accordingly.

In some ways, the swing toward "belonging" is a direct response to cold, uncaring, all-business organizations. In fact, that's what makes it so seductive to certain employees who were traumatized by prior workplaces. They have soaring expectations when promised a sense of family. I've even seen instances when they were looking for a feeling of belonging that even their actual families didn't provide. Consciously or not, it's a psychological manipulation to let employees believe they're going to get the things from work that they didn't get from their actual family. Of course, people are very disgruntled when that doesn't happen. Overpromising what a company can offer its workforce raises the stakes in a way that is almost certain to boomerang.

Levels of Community

Setting up Sounding Board involved cultivating a very particular form of community. Our business is built around working with a network of coaches—hundreds of them, all independent vendors with their own practices, across the globe. We wanted to create a sense of connection among these coaches and with Sounding Board.

We felt it was important to offer a sense of community because independent practitioners of coaching often are solo practitioners. And they don't necessarily have a community to tap into. Right from the start, we create a cohort when they join the network, so everyone has a small group of people they're connected with. We have required community meetings quarterly. We organize educational events. We've set up a system so coaches in our network can ask for advice from fellow coaches, as well as practice groups so they can discuss their difficult cases, and so on.

We try to offer ways to have coaches find small communities within the larger Sounding Board community—sometimes according to their specialty or where they're based. This is really key, because otherwise it's easy to feel like just one among the masses, like a student who graduates from a small high school and struggles at a large university unless they can find some smaller community to attach to. All our coaches work remotely, and, of course, most of them have never met one another in person, but we've seen real friendships emerge, as well as many professional collaborations.

These activities help coaches make connections within the network, but they also connect the network to Sounding Board, which is just as important. In fact, we also offer coaches stock options as a method to deepen their connection to the company and its success. We are the only company in our industry to do this, and we do it because it helps connect our coach community and our business community together. So coaches have their coaching in common, and perhaps the accreditation school they're connected to, but they have Sounding Board in common, too. And all those connections are reinforcing.

It's important to underscore that we didn't *force* a sense of community. We identified opportunities to enable a sense of community. So it's still connection, not belonging, and not family. We've set all this up so that what you put in, you get out. The more hours of coaching you put in for Sounding Board, the more you get out; the

> *It's important to underscore that we didn't* force *a sense of community. We identified opportunities to enable a sense of community.*

more you contribute to the community, the more you get out; the longer you stay, the more you get. It's very much a balanced equation.

So Close You Can't See Anything

The pervasive confusion around the line between belonging and work is not just an issue with rank-and-file employees. Leaders can become susceptible, too. I have some version of this conversation with practically every leader I coach. "Wait a minute, this is work," I'll have to remind them. "This is just work. You're choosing to be there. You don't have the same level of obligation to work that you have to, say, your children, or your own health. You are getting too close to work."

Here's how I help them think about it—and this applies not just to top leaders but to everyone trying to keep a proper perspective on work.

Open up your hand and rest your palm on the tip of your nose. Try to look at your hand, and all you can see is a big blur, with some abstract colors poking through in the background. You can't see any of the detail of your hand, and you can't really comprehend what's behind and beyond it.

But if you move your hand back a foot or so from your nose, just the length of your personal space, then you can see all the detail on your palm, and you can see what's beyond it as well.

When you think of work as family, it's like having your hand against your nose: Your view is compromised. Therefore, your decisions are compromised. Therefore, you're compromising yourself. You are holding work too closely.

So you have to create a little space between you and work to actually be able to observe. But too many companies, intentionally or not, try to get people to have work right up against the nose—pressing, so they'll do *anything* for the job. This actually doesn't help the company, precisely because that person's perceptions are compromised. They have a narrow, unclear view.

It can be even worse for leaders, because when you get to the leadership level, you are *committed*. I have had a coachee say, "I got another job offer for a higher title and twice as much money, but I can't leave."

"Why can't you leave?" I ask.

"I can't leave my team. That would be a betrayal," they respond.

You can see how this is kind of insidious. And I think as a result of both the pandemic and the younger generation coming into the workforce, more people are saying, "Work is something I do. It's not who I am. It's not my original family." Which is healthier in the long run for everybody.

> *More people are saying: "Work is something I do. It's not who I am. It's not my original family."*

Beyond the Third Right Answer

We started this dive into cultivating connection with a binary dynamic: business or family? But as is clear by now, exploring the fuller context offers up a whole range of potential options and reframings. Any final decisions about a specific strategy will depend on the details and goals of a specific organization, but obviously we have a lot more options now than we did at the beginning of the process.

I'll close this discussion with just a couple more observations—one fairly specific, the other a big-picture point.

First the nitty-gritty one. Among the core capabilities a leader must cultivate is *leading a high-performing team*. Google spent five years doing a study that identified five qualities of high-performing teams.[1] I'll quote the top three:

1. **Psychological safety:** Can we take risks on this team without feeling insecure or embarrassed?

2. **Dependability:** Can we count on each other to do high-quality work on time?

3. **Structure and clarity:** Are goals, roles, and execution plans on our team clear?

The other two qualities addressed the meaning and impact of the team's work. But I think these top three can be summarized in a way that clarifies the difference between effective team-building and the unrealistic goal of "belonging":

High-performing teams have a sense of community and trust.

High-performing teams have a sense of community and trust.

This draws on other capabilities, like inclusiveness, but the point is that it's something a leader can cultivate. And it's a frame that gets beyond binary thinking.

When you think it through, this really isn't about belonging or not belonging. It's about a gradation of the idea of belonging, what it can mean depending on how it's defined, and understanding how a workplace can or can't deliver it. Likely the third right answer will entail some blending of community, belonging, and the work context. But the real lesson is that there is never just a single third right answer. That's why cultivating the ability to surface multiple options is so vital. And it's also why—when the time comes to make real choices—developing judgment is vital, too. It's not about merely trying to avoid failure, because by now you know failure can be learned from and overcome. There are many third right answers. You can find them. And you can choose. It's up to you to make the

The third right answer will entail some blending of community, belonging, and the work context.

decision what is the best answer for your environment, in your context, with your skills and capabilities, in this moment. No one can tell you the right answer. It's the hard, courageous work of leadership. How to make it real is your decision. Now you have to make the choice! And thank goodness, you can have the help of a neutral leadership coach and thinking partner to help.

Coach: I'm guessing you are already doing some of these things that promote community at work. What could you add?

1. **Identify a Common Interest, Purpose, or Passion:** This leads to a shared commitment. Working at the same company provides a common interest. Articulating and sharing advances the larger purpose or passion the company is engaged in.

2. **Common Values:** Name the values the community is built on. But go further: It's about living those values out in your culture and your business decisions.

3. **Common Norms (Preferably Stated):** Often companies have unstated norms that exclude those who do not guess or pick up on them. Even if norms remain unstated (it's hard to name them all), members should serve as "ambassadors" to help newcomers understand "this is how we do things here."

4. **Promote Interaction:** The real magic of a community starts happening when members build connections with each other. Satisfaction is increased when people find new friendships, professional connections, and opportunities to collaborate. Find ways to gather, whether virtual or in person. (All these community-building ideas can work virtually: The online world is full of thriving communities; your work community thrive can be, too.)

5. **Collaboration/Shared Learning:** Spark collaboration through shared learning—whether provided by the company or by community members.

6. **Appreciation/Acknowledgment:** Appreciating community participation goes a long way toward increasing engagement.

7. **Trust/Respect:** Although this is the basis of every community, it nevertheless needs to be named. Without trust and respect, facilitating an environment in which members take care of each other while accepting people's differences is impossible. Addressing members' concerns promptly and sensitively adds to the sense of welcome, and safety.

8. **Fun:** People want to enjoy themselves in a community. So even though it is work, finding ways to have fun together is key.

Coach: What's the first step toward implementing this idea?

Why Context Is Key

I know how to solve this problem. I did it when I was a junior manager at my last company.

Coach: Maybe. But you might want to think twice.

What? Why?

Coach: You're now a senior leader at a different company. Everything has changed.

Back when I worked for a training firm, we would follow up sessions by subsequently asking participants to evaluate the experience they'd had. In part we referenced what's known as the Kirkpatrick Model. To simplify, we asked which of the following responses applied:

1. I liked the training.
2. I learned somcething from it.
3. I could use what I learned in my work.
4. I have already put what I learned into practice.

The vast majority of evaluations stopped at "I liked it." Many said they'd learned something, a few said it was something they could imagine using. Almost nobody arrived at the final stage, having actually applied what they'd learned.

That's the problem with traditional training. All this useful information is shared, all manner of genuinely helpful skills are taught, but often it is prepackaged with the same skill set applied to every person on the whole planet. It lacks context. Without the contextual element, people frequently can't apply it.

From the start—even before I became a coach—I was fixated on that last category. The training firm I worked for had an award for the trainer whose evaluations showed they could translate the skills training to actual usage. I won that award, because actual usage was always my main focus and goal. The way I saw it, if it couldn't be used in the real work context and right away, it didn't matter how brilliant what I taught was. Most likely, the new skill will fall off and the training will prove a waste of time. And I really hate wasting time, my own or others'.

I now liken it to language learning. I've been studying Spanish. After class, if I don't use whatever I learned within 24 hours, it just doesn't stick. It's the same with Tai Chi, actually. A lot of the practice is learning movements, and we always recommend that students practice what they've learned within 24 hours, because if you don't do it right away, you lose it. You'll come back to class the next week and feel like you missed something, like some core part of what you learned has just disappeared from your brain, because you haven't applied your new skill or knowledge in context. Application is what makes the learning stick.

Over time, I understood that this was the value, and the potential, of good coaching. When it's done right, coaching is the opposite of off-the-shelf training: It's personalized and individualized. It's designed to take on questions about how to use skills and capabilities in this particular context, or in that particular situation. You could think of this as the third level that builds on what we've covered so far in this section: not just acquiring skills, and not just learning how to combine them into capabilities that encompass whole sets of skills. Applying the right capability to a particular context at the right time is what adds up to success.

> *Applying the right capability to a particular context at the right time is what adds up to success.*

Traditional training generally only hits the first level, or perhaps the second. But it's seldom about applying something in a real-world, specific context. And without addressing a concrete application followed through in context, trainees don't really own their new skills. They haven't integrated it into the way they operate.

I sensed that context was key back in my training days, but it really became clearer to me what to do about that later as my own context changed.

Who Is in the Context

As much as I believed in a focus on teaching skills that could be applied right away when I was in leadership training, the real value of understanding context sank in when I moved into coaching.

Looking back, I was actually kind of arrogant in the beginning. I thought I knew what my clients should do. They'd describe a situation and dilemma, and I'd draw on my experience dealing with all kinds of companies and scenarios and say: "Oh, here's something you could do in that situation." And in my defense, this is exactly what clients wanted; as we've already seen. There's an endless appetite for "just tell me what to do" solutions. So I'd dip into my deep well of knowledge and suggest a course of action. And they'd go do it.

Then they'd come back and say it didn't work out, or even that it blew up in their face. I was startled. What went wrong? Why didn't it work? And invariably they'd explain that it was because of this detail, or that specific person, the subtleties of the company's culture, or some other element of the particular situation that I couldn't have been fluent in. They were rarely upset with me, though, because they realized, in retrospect, that I didn't know the entire context. Only they did.

I learned from that and adjusted accordingly. I had to drop the vestiges of my "training mind" attitude: Here's the set of skills, just apply them. Because it didn't work that way. The reality is: The client is in the context. I am not there.

That really informed my coaching approach, and oriented it toward the idea of offering a set of potential options, and pushing it back to the coachee: What do you think will work best in your context?

This personalized things in a useful way, but of course it's still not a magic bullet. The coachee will still have misfires and learn over time. But they'll learn more quickly; dispensing with generic solutions and becoming more context-specific creates an accelerated success pathway. Just what is needed when the time frame for leader development has become so compressed.

But on a deeper level, this entails an important new challenge: Really learning to understand your context.

Coaching in Context

Part of our process at Sounding Board includes regular (virtual) gatherings of coaches in our network to explore best practices. The importance of context is a recurring theme, but there was one instance in particular that left an impression that's useful to share here.

As part of the session, one of our most seasoned coaches had a discussion with a newer coach, who had an upcoming first meeting with a top executive at a major pharma company. The veteran coach shared all the prep work he does. It wasn't just a Google search on the company and a look at the executive's LinkedIn profile. It was listening to the company earnings calls, looking at the public financials, getting up to speed on the sector, setting up a news alert on the company name to keep abreast of new developments, reading culture docs. In other words, he was trying to get a sense of the context.

But the newer coach wasn't fully convinced. Her concern, in fact, was knowing *too much* about her client's business. Wouldn't that ruin her role as neutral observer? Wouldn't her responses come across as her take on her client's business, and in effect telling him what she would do? It was practically an "ignorance is bliss" argument.

Ignorance may be bliss, but it's not a helpful stance for a coach. It's true that you shouldn't slide into the consultant role of saying "Here's what I'd do, or here's what you should do." But you can avoid that trap while remaining fully informed of the client's context. In fact, you *must* do precisely that to be a good coach. Understanding context doesn't mean passing judgments, giving advice, or thinking you know what the client should do. It means understanding more about the world in which the client is operating.

Unfortunately, many coaches are trained to strive for the uninformed (ignorant) version of "neutrality." They're trained to believe you don't need to know anything about context, or the client's environment. In fact, they end up thinking it's better if they don't know, because they think they will be more neutral. And it's possible that's true for a life coach, dealing with a spousal dispute or something along those lines, but it's not true for a leadership coach.

A much more sophisticated approach is to take in all the information you can—and *still* be neutral. This is far more difficult and is a good example of applying the unity of the opposites approach. Gathering that information isn't so the coach can tell the client what to do. Rather, it enables you to help them succeed in their context, a context you have taken the time to try to understand. Context makes all the difference.

On the Levels

No matter how much homework you do, the tricky part of coaching someone in context is that only *they* can know their context in full. Even then, not every coachee "gets" their own context in full at first. I can give a client a menu of options, but if they're overlooking some element of their context, they aren't going to make the best decisions.

No matter how much homework you do, the tricky part of coaching someone in context is that only they can know their context in full.

More specifically, one of the common problems is that they often misinterpret their context. We all have our internal biases, and one of the most powerful and commonplace is overpersonalizing or focusing on just one element of your context. Let's say the problem is a colleague taking a certain action that causes you problems. "It's because they don't like me! They're trying to get my job! They're mean, they don't care about the company," and so on. You can fill in the blanks. There are always plenty of easy-to-imagine *personal* reasons that somebody did something. This can obviously really throw off your understanding of your actual context.

I'll say more later about dealing with this specific bias, but the big picture is that coaching can help with context by helping coachees elevate their thinking out of the personal, and into a broader organizational context.

One of our basic principles at Sounding Board is to coach the person in the context of their leadership role.

One of our basic principles at Sounding Board is to coach the person in the context of their leadership role. In many scenarios that means setting aside personal interpretations, and thinking: "I'm going to view this as a leader, within a broader organizational view. How does that perspective change my potential response?"

Leaders often get stalled because their contextual view doesn't keep up as they advance in their careers. Even otherwise

Leaders often get stalled because their contextual view doesn't keep up as they move through their careers.

successful leaders get stuck thinking like individual contributors—the way they rose through the ranks in the first place—and that it's all about them personally. Instead, they should be thinking like organizational leaders. The coach's role is to prod them to take in a contextual view based on the correct level of leadership.

At each level of leadership, the contextual view gets broader and broader.

Think of a particular capability such as strategic planning. If you're an individual contributor, you're going to be looking at that from a certain perspective. But that's very different from how you're going to be thinking about executing strategic planning as the CFO.

A first step, then, in understanding context is up-leveling your views, so you're looking at a situation in a broader way. Maybe it's inevitable that we start by thinking about a problem or challenge in a personal way. But the next level might be viewing it from the perspective of a team dynamic. And the next place beyond that might be viewing it from your functional area dynamic, and next from the perspective of a cross-functional dynamic. Finally, from the view of the entire company dynamic. And for a top-level executive, you're also looking beyond the organization, at the competition, the industry, the market, and the broader macroeconomic environment. At each level of leadership, the contextual view gets broader and broader.

Culture Clashes

But that's not the only challenge in understanding context. The details of those perspectives from different levels can also vary quite a bit from company to company. Every organization operates in its own unique way. That's organizational culture. And culture matters—especially when you're dealing with a new (to you) culture, or a culture that's in flux. (And increasingly, *all* organizational cultures are evolving thanks to shifts in the broader workplace.)

I'll give you some examples of how this context can matter, and I'll start with one where the culture issue is particularly easy to visualize. I once had a coaching client who was a top executive at a high-growth and very innovative tech startup. At the time, this company had fewer than a thousand employees and was maybe five years old. It was merging with a company in the same general category that had 100,000 employees and dated back a century.

You can imagine that the approach to leadership would be very different in these two distinct company cultures. That can be a real challenge for a leader who has established a thriving career in one specific context. It's human nature to think, "Well, I've made this whole series of decisions that have worked out well. Why should I change?"

This is true, by the way, for leaders going in the other direction, jumping from massive organizations to lean startups. I've had clients like that, too, and the challenge is fundamentally the same: What made us successful previously is what we want to keep doing. That's our system; it's what success looks like. "This whole record of decisions has gotten me so far, so surely that will prove to be true again."

But of course that's not how it works. And this particular client knew it: He really wanted to learn his new context. Success, he understood, would look different in this new culture.

That culture difference, in this case, had an obvious manifestation. When leadership teams from the merger partners met, it was obvious who came from which culture. One group (from the bigger and more venerable company) wore dark suits, white shirts, and ties. The ones from the startup showed up in jeans, T-shirts, and sneakers.

Now, as we covered early in this book, I have direct experience with the connection between company culture and dress norms. Silly as it can seem, it's a real company culture signal—not an insurmountable one, but one you can't just ignore. So I pointed out to my client that if he kept up with the jeans and T-shirts, the execs from the other side of the merger would never fully accept him, and would never take him seriously. "You don't have to *be* them," I suggested. "But if you want to fit into this new cultural context, you might have to take a step closer to them."

He started wearing a suit with a colorful dress shirt and colorful socks (no tie) to those meetings. This became a metaphor for his whole approach to this new context: I'm accommodating your culture, but I'm from this other culture. In other words, he didn't have to become another person. But he did have to truly understand the context that he was operating in.

Sometimes that's not possible, and the new culture really *does* require you to become a person you don't want to be. But in all cases, the context is key. Truly understanding the context is the only way to make the right choices for you.

That client ended up being one of the only leaders from his startup to survive its merger. The reason he made it through, happily, is that he accepted a basic truth that most people miss: "Hey, wait a minute—my context has changed!"

Stay or Go

A merger can be a particularly intense culture collision and context shift, but leaders can encounter similar challenges just by changing jobs. Research shows that between 25% and 33% of newly hired leaders leave before they hit the one-year mark.

I did a lot of coaching at a top Fortune 100 company that I'll call Acme Corp. Their culture was very amiable and very people oriented. When I walked down the hall at Acme HQ, everyone said hello, asked me if I needed help, and generally welcomed me.

However, Acme kept hiring people from another major firm—I'll call it Ace Inc.—which was one of the most aggressive and hard-driving companies of its time. It was *super* cutthroat. Those Ace people would get into Acme and right away make enemies and step on everyone's toes. Of course they were only trying to be successful in the style they knew from Ace, but this did not work in the Acme culture.

So my contacts at Acme called me and said, "Oh my God, you gotta fix these people we hired from Ace! They're too aggressive. They're too domineering, too demanding."

Of course I could not "fix" these Ace veterans in the sense of somehow magically turning them into Acme naturals. But I understood the request. The Ace approach was not working in the Acme context and causing attrition on both sides. This created increased cost, lack of direction, and uncertainty, as well as a retention problem, for Acme. It was a bad situation for the Ace veterans, too—even if their hard-driving tactics worked in the short term, they were probably leaving a raft of enemies in their wake and undermining their long-term success at Acme.

What I *could* do was help them understand they were in a different context and how to operate in this context versus the context that they came from.

About 80% of the time, they wanted to shift and operate in that new context, now that they understood the difference. And about 20% of the time, they said, "This is just not me. Dialing it back and being amiable—I can't do it." And that's fair. It just means it's time to look for another job that offers the kind of culture they could thrive in. One of the main reasons people leave any given job isn't that they don't have the skills or expertise or they dislike the actual work—it's because they're not a cultural fit. So the sooner you can get a leader or potential leader to truly engage with their context, the better.

The Mantra Method

It takes conscious effort and dedicated thought to understand your context. You have to find ways to step back and really pay attention to things that you've been taking for granted. Our view, our contextual view, is embedded in the brain. It's like a neural pathway, and those pathways are hard to change. Sometimes, I've discovered, it helps to give clients a simple mantra—one that helps forge a new neural pathway that allows them to achieve a fresh view of their context.

Think of it like paving a road. If an old, existing road starts to develop cracks and potholes, you can fill them in. But we all know that only works for a little while; the next storm comes and that pothole reemerges. You have to pave over that whole road, ideally a bunch of times to solve the problem. And one way to change your perception is by layering on new ways of thinking; it's not the only way, but it's one strategy for changing your contextual thinking.

To do this, I use what I call a mantra. It's not a spiritual mantra. It's a phrase you repeat to yourself over and over again, until you've laid down enough asphalt that the old road underneath isn't showing.

One mantra I have used regularly with leaders changing companies is "That was then, this is now." The goal is to bring them present into the current context while not disregarding or diminishing their past roles. It's so simple, yet powerfully effective.

One of my favorite mantras is directly related to the "levels" theme I discussed earlier—making a shift from individual contributor to frontline manager. It sounds simple: "It's not about me."

Frequently a new client will start out treating coaching sessions as an opportunity to just rehash their existing perceptions: to complain about someone's actions or some difficult turn of events. First, as I described in Chapter 5, I'll try to get them to acknowledge and help them name how they're feeling about this—betrayed, angry, irritated, whatever the case may be. But then it's often helpful to introduce a mantra: some simple, consistent idea that they can revisit and that will always help them reframe.

In this case: "It's not about me." That's simple, but it's a mental shift. Your job, your role, your career, is no longer just about you. It's about the team now. I often literally tell clients that anytime anything troublesome or challenging happens, they have to say that phrase to themselves. "It's not about me."

Once it's not about you, what are your thoughts about what is happening in the team? They'll immediately see something different: the broader context. That person's comment in that meeting (or whatever the short-term problem was) makes a whole other kind of sense—because of the context.

To take this mantra example one step further, and make it even more concrete: I've heard so many times some version of "That employee just doesn't care! They just don't care about anything!"

I'll say something like, "Okay, that could be true. But we don't know if it's true." It could be that the employee feels discouraged. Maybe they're not getting any positive feedback. Maybe they think they're failing. Or they don't know how to do the job they've been given, and they are afraid to let anybody know that because they might get fired—or whatever it might be. I'll give four or five different perspectives.

"Any of those resonate with you?" I'll ask. "Any of those seem plausible?"

Suddenly there's a shift. Instead of fixating on how that employee bothers them, they'll shift (it's not about me) to examining the context. "Yeah, you know, actually, that person missed their onboarding. So maybe they actually don't know everything they need to"—or some other light will come on.

You can move a problem out of a place that you have no control over and into a place where you can address it as a leader.

After all, if the employee really doesn't care, that's out of your control; you can't make them care. But if they don't know what their job is; they're discouraged; they have too many failures; they have someone blocking them; they don't have the resources, support, or teammates—all those are things a leader can do something about.

That's the essence of what you can gain from understanding context: You can move a problem out of a place that you have no control over and into a place where you can address the issue as a leader.

All coaching should address context, but that doesn't always happen. Especially in the early years of the coaching industry, the practice was sometimes geared more toward simply helping and encouraging the client to achieve some particular goal that they had come up with. Maybe they wanted to become the leader of a specific team. Instead of exploring the context—is that the right goal for what you really really want?—they would just try to bowl everyone over, with their coach functioning more like a strategic cheerleader. People would wonder, "What happened to this person?"

Leadership Coaching works when it addresses how what the individual wants (really wants) overlaps with the context of the organization. If you can't find that sweet spot, then either the organization is unhappy or the individual is unhappy. Luckily, quite frequently you can find the sweet spot.

> *Coaching works when it addresses how what the individual wants (really wants) overlaps with the context of the organization.*

In the early days of my current company, Sounding Board, there was some pressure to define a very specific leadership philosophy for our customers—to articulate "this is the best kind of leader." I refused. I said, "If we do that, then only the companies that have that style of leadership will want to work with us. We have to do the opposite. We have to show that we will coach leaders in the context of their company, in the culture that they have, in the style of leadership they want, in relation to who they are." That was the right message for the emerging context around coaching itself.

> *We will coach leaders in the context of their company, in the culture that they have, in the style of leadership they want, in relation to who they are.*

Context as Opportunity

Many of the examples I've given about understanding context are about reacting—to a problem, to a career change, to a culture shift. But context is also key to *acting:* spotting, understanding, and taking advantage of opportunities that you might otherwise have overlooked. This is important, and in fact, it's at the core of how Sounding Board itself came to exist.

Here's the backstory. Somewhere around 2010, one of my coaching clients was the new CEO of a promising startup. I coached him during a volatile period, and things worked out well, and the growth of the company really took off. So this client wanted me to coach a couple of his up-and-coming executives as well. Normally I'd just refer those clients to some-one else in my trusted network of coaches—to avoid any poten-tial conflicts—but he really wanted me to do it. We talked through my concerns and ultimately I agreed. One of those up-and-comers was Christine Tao.

Christine had been with the company for just a couple of years, but she had rapidly risen to senior vice-president. She was already doing extremely well, but the coaching was really pro-ductive on top of that—she ended up being responsible for something like 60% of the company's business as it rapidly grew toward Unicorn status.

That engagement ran its course. Fast forward a few years and I had moved on to new clients, and then to my adventure joining and helping build a new startup. One day, Christine called. She had left that company and wanted to start something new—a coaching company. "Coaching was the best professional develop-ment I ever had," she said, "And I think more people should have access to it." Of course, she did not have a background as a coach herself—she was in sales—and the idea was still a work in pro-gress; she'd put a lot of thought and time into it, but hadn't incor-porated. Would I, she asked, be interested in working on it with her?

I thought about what I knew of the context around coaching, and how it was evolving. Certainly it had moved past the early days when it was a "behind closed doors" proposition, seen as mostly used for derailed executives.

So many executives I'd coached had told me, "I wish I'd had access to this earlier in my career. It's really useful now but it would have been amazing when I was a new manager or middle manager." Or "I would have moved up to VP much faster, because that transition is a tough one!" So clearly there was a need.

Still, just a few years earlier, I probably would have turned aside Christine's outreach. Of course, I agreed with those clients about the potential for coaching to help a wider range of junior and potential and midlevel leaders. But it was still largely a C-suite proposition.

The real difference, though, was that *my* context had changed, too. I had been on the front lines of a startup that had succeeded in the venture capital process, and I had learned that I really enjoyed the process of building something new. Despite the challenge, I was ready for a new big leap.

"Okay," I said, "let's do it." We incorporated in 2016. My other startup was winding down, so for about six months I was doing double duty (plus keeping a small number of coaching clients) and sleeping minimal hours a night. But I knew it was the right decision—because of the context.

The Coaching Context

We believed there was a need—but we also thought it was the right timing. And just getting the timing right, it turns out, is one of the key factors of startup success. (That prior startup I'd been part of, which focused on virtual reality, was probably ahead of its time.) Also, we recognized how technology changes, and work-culture shifts were changing the larger context of leadership in ways that we could make the most of.

For starters, more companies were seeing the broader benefits of coaching, but were having mixed results integrating into their more traditional human resources and training functions. The process of finding an effective coach match can be complicated and time-consuming, especially if the task basically fell to an HR worker with other responsibilities and no particular expertise in the coaching field; the best estimate at the time was that only about half of such coaching arrangements were judged successful. I recently heard from an HR partner of mine that the success of those early coaching engagements was more like 20%.

The main reason coaching was still seen as being only for the executive level was the cost. That cost included a lot of personal attention and travel, because of an expectation that executives needed in-person sessions. To address that challenge, we did two things. We made our coaching virtual—which, of course, would have been impossible a decade prior.

Secondly, we put everything that could be automated on a technology platform. So instead of having a face-to-face first meeting—in which potential clients answer questions about who they are and their expectations for the coaching—we automated that with a survey. We could also do away with "chemistry meetings," in which a coach and potential client talked for an hour to see if they were a fit. Instead, we created a matching algorithm to connect coaches and coachees. We are about 95% successful on the first match, which is amazing and saves everyone time and money.

We got our initial seed funding at the end of 2017, and launched early the next year. The biggest pushback early on was that coaching wouldn't work virtually, but then the pandemic hit and the context changed. We all learned that practically *everything* can work virtually. And companies started to see the advantages—flexibility, lower cost, privacy, and so on.

We also knew that we could quickly build out a network of coaches who could come on as contractors to add to their own practices and benefit from being associated with Sounding Board and its methods and capabilities. I'd been in the industry for over 20 years, so I knew a lot of people. But the real key was that we could strike mutually beneficial arrangements with hundreds of quality coaches, because we truly understood their context.

At the time there was one other virtual coaching company. In a way, this helped, because it gave proof of concept to the category, and it gave us an existing standard to differentiate from—by design. (Their model was more centered on all-purpose coaching—life coaching, mental health, and so on—while we zeroed in on leadership.) We've also concentrated on a tighter, more closely aligned network of coaches who coach in the Sounding Board way, and are committed to a larger number of Sounding Board engagements. That's part of the sense of community I discussed in Chapter 8. But it's also about con-

> *We were in a position to both participate in and accelerate a revolution in leadership development.*

text: We want coaches to coach in the Sounding Board way because that makes the coaching experience consistent across the customer company.

There's one last big-picture bit of context that tied all of this together, and made us confident: We were in a position to both participate in and accelerate a revolution in leadership development. When I started coaching back in the 1990s, the dominant clients were large enterprise companies built around a development model that workers would spend their entire career at one firm. Within a decade, that started to change. By the time Christine approached me about starting a business that could truly deliver the benefits of leadership coaching at scale, the work landscape was different.

> *The opening was to take a lead role in inventing—through coaching that responds to the contemporary technological and cultural context—a new model.*

People started changing jobs like crazy, and the typical tenure dropped down to something closer to three to five years. As we've seen earlier in this book, the whole old-school model of leader development no longer was functional, but many companies were clinging to it anyway. The opening was to take a lead role in inventing—through coaching that responds to the contemporary technological and cultural context—a new model. That would mean not just adjusting to this new context, but helping to shape it—with new tools, new metrics, new ways of developing leaders. And, as we'll explore in the final section, that's what we've set out to do.

Coach: So you're interested in understanding your context more deeply? Here are some ways to do that.

1. Listen or think deeply to identify root or underlying causes or needs. These tend to be unspoken/unwritten.

2. Question any thinking, assumptions, or rationalizations that you are attributing to others ("They don't care").

3. Identify implied or inferred relationships to be sure they are accurate. (It's easy to assume that if A is the case, then B must be true. But are you sure? Or are you making an assumption?)

4. Decide how to think about a problem by actively choosing a perspective (or two) from which to view it.

5. Clarify what you want to have happen—what is the desired outcome? How does this meet your larger purpose or values?

6. Restate or reframe the problem. (A coach can help you do this.)

Coach: Which approach would you like to use more regularly? How will you make sure you do that?

PART

III

Impact

Lasting Change

> *Actually, things have been going really well lately. I made some missteps, but I learned from them and now I feel like I'm on course.*
>
> **Coach: It's true. You're on a roll.**
>
> *So what happens now?*
>
> **Coach: Now we focus on how you keep that going, despite the challenges you can't see coming.**

On some fundamental level, leadership development involves change. Whether you're talking about an up-and-coming manager with aspirations and potential, or a seasoned executive at the peak of their career, success is always about adjusting, improving, growing. That's what good coaching can help with.

Success is always about adjusting, improving, growing. That's what good coaching can help with.

The opening section of this book, much like a typical coaching engagement, established why there is a need to do something different. Leadership development has gotten hung up on old ways from past decades that just don't apply anymore. The middle section—and again, this echoes a coaching cycle—zeroed in, with greater and greater practical detail, on what needs to be different, and the specific ways to figure that out and accept the changes and challenges it requires. All of which leads up to truly understanding context.

That brings us to the final section: Here's what leaders and aspiring leaders can do differently. In a coaching sequence, that means not only addressing whatever particular issue might have inspired the coaching engagement in the first place, but equipping the coachee with capacity to meet the next challenge, and the one after that, beyond the end of the coaching engagement. That's what the finale of the book aims to do, too.

Over the prior nine chapters, we've spelled out the context of the current revolution in leadership development, leading up to coaching as a key leader development tool—not just its popularity, but it's potential. In the final three, we'll spell out the advantages of coaching over more traditional training approaches of the past: the contextual elements, the way it can be personalized and individualized, how it can be both shaped to the moment and fit into a pattern of continuous development. It represents a break from training that's so common to standard leader development programs.

This final section will delve into the specifics of what that means and what new methods are taking shape as a result—including our development of a new Leader Success model, and a long-needed reinvention of performance evaluations, among other innovations. In short, the objective of this final section is not just to explain why coaching has become so popular, but to establish why it needs to expand more and more in the future, into the fabric of employee development and the culture of corporations.

The Democratization of Complexity

While many of my executive-level clients told me they wished they'd had access to coaching earlier in their career, that by itself wasn't enough to justify the effort to found a company dedicated to widening access to coaching and its methods. There wasn't just a *wish* for such access. There was a *need*. That was true even before we started Sounding Board, but it's become even clearer since we launched.

One reason coaching was mostly limited to the level of vice presidents or higher was due to the complexity involved in that level of leadership. The issues are very complicated, multileveled, and nuanced. It takes a true thinking partner to try to take that complexity apart enough to figure out what its components are, what the consequences might be, what the context is, what needs to happen.

What's changed over the past decade or so . . . is that leaders at all levels routinely face this same level of complexity.

What's changed over the past decade or so—and this has certainly accelerated in the past five years—is that leaders at all levels routinely face this same level of complexity. Even if you're a supervisor on a production floor, you have to manage issues around race, gender, and equity. You have safety issues, performance-measurement issues, development issues, hiring issues, retention issues. Lately, you might have to contend with remote work or hybrid-office issues, too. Not to mention issues around workplace violence. And all of that is on top of the job you were actually hired to do, which itself has become more complex thanks to economic and environmental uncertainty, politics, supply-chain issues, new technology, competition, and on and on.

So many of these obligations and issues used to be handled at the top of the company. Now, all of that is getting handled at every level of in the company. That really wasn't true in the past. Back then, folks at the top would come down with some set of rules and decisions, and then you would just implement whatever they were. (That's why so many C-suite leaders needed coaching!) But now facing these issues happens for every leader, at every level.

And even if HR says, "This is what we're doing about equity," it doesn't matter if someone in your group concludes something inequitable is happening. You can say "This is what the company does to ensure equitable treatment," but that hardly solves the issue at hand.

The upshot is that frontline managers and leaders all the way up to the top are having direct contact with navigating the complexity of the current work environment. That is dramatically different than in the past. And it's a context that requires a dramatically different response.

> *Frontline managers and leaders all the way up to the top are having direct contact with navigating the complexity of the current work environment.*

Don't Hire a Soccer Coach to Teach Tennis

We realized this right away, but we also realized that the right response would partly entail a challenge for us, too. We were building a major network of coaches to properly meet this previously overlooked demand. And there were plenty who could adjust to the new world. But for some coaches who were long used to working with C-suite executives almost exclusively, it was a new challenge to work with a broader range of leaders across an organization.

So we train them—specifically addressing the context of coaching leaders at different levels. While the complexities at different levels may be equally numerous and wide-ranging, they're also distinct. The resources and skill sets for leaders at different levels are specific. You can't coach that frontline supervisor the same way you're going to coach the C-suite exec.

We recognize that using the same coaching strategy and approach at every tier just won't work, because of varied context. While complexity is more widespread now, leadership still operates differently at different levels. So we work to define: here's what decision-making looks like at a junior tier, here's what it looks like at the middle tier, here's how it looks at the top. Different contexts require a different approach.

Think of it this way: You're not going to coach, an athlete who is making their first run at competing on a regional level the same way you're going to coach an Olympic champion. Yes, a competitor at a state tournament and someone defending her Australian Open title have a common objective—defeating their opponent—but the details are going to be very different. It's the same with coaching leaders.

Our approach on this front is distinct in the broader coaching field. We offer coaches in our network post-certification training specifically focused on leadership coaching at multiple levels, with the goal of matching leaders with the right thinking partner. What we don't do—and this is a path others have chosen—is branch out to offer different varieties of coaching (life coaching, mental health, etc.) and treat "leadership" as a single, interchangeable category that works across all levels.

Specialization is important and is only getting more so. If you're training to win at tennis, don't rely on a soccer coach! You want someone who understands your context. So we have a set of principles for how you coach leaders and it has made a big difference for us in two ways. First, the developmental impact of more specialized coaching is far greater. Second, having a set of principles creates consistency across the customer company, so that all leaders are being coached in the same structure even though the details are personalized. We think of it like a coordinated picture wall. All the frames are the same black material but the paintings inside the frame, painted by the coach and their client, are all unique. We set out to help grow coaches who would in turn help grow leaders. This approach was and remains based on our observation of today's leadership context—and our read on *tomorrow*'s leadership context as well.

Coach First

I've noted from the start that an effective coaching engagement does not begin—as many assume—with a lot of "getting to know you" time. To the contrary, it starts by seeking to identify, right away, the "big leap" that a coachee needs to take. That, as you will recall, is where this book began: No throat-clearing, let's get to the main event. A good coaching relationship starts exactly the same way. Sure, there are plenty of coaches out there who still spend a session or two on the formalities of acquaintance, but we think that's largely wasted time.

Instead, it's better to quickly identify a topic, and start coaching from the first session—landing on the big leap that will be the goal and set the tone for the rest of the cycle. This way you're giving the client a direct experience of what to expect and how it can help: "So that was an example of coaching. What do you think?," a coach might say.

Partly this is just more efficient, and a good mental jump-start that most clients appreciate. But it's also a better way to do exactly what those "getting to know you" conversations are supposedly about: establishing trust. Many people (even many coaches) think trust develops over time, and that it's based on a feeling of safety. In other words, the coach's job would be to project: "I don't judge you; I listen to everything you have to say." But a better way to develop trust is by talking about the tough things, and getting through them together. We think trust develops by confronting issues that the coachee is facing, honestly. So we just start doing that right from the beginning. Sometimes the coachee is surprised by this approach—but in the end they almost always appreciate it.[1]

Coach (Only) Leadership

This sounds obvious, but it can actually be a significant issue. Earlier I mentioned that, as a company, we focus on leadership coaching, period. Mental health, parenting, other varieties of coaching all have their value, but that's not what we do. This holds true within the coaching engagement, too.

For example, an organization might position coaching as something closer to mental health— a response to worries about burnout and stress. Leadership coaching isn't about learning how to de-stress! Depending on the specific scenario, it may be that the issue can be reframed: As a leader, part of your job is learning to manage your stress. Because you're a responsible leader; stress is a given! So how do you manage it for yourself and for the people around you so that you're not *spreading* stress or letting your stress impact your performance (or your health, because how can you lead if you are sick)?

Similarly, individual clients may (consciously or unconsciously) try to steer sessions on to other, non leadership terrain. This is not good for anybody. A leadership coach is not there to serve as a marriage counselor or a therapist. The focus is leadership; everything we do is in that context.

Now, it's possible that a client's divorce or parenting challenges or other personal issues are impacting their leadership. Or it may be the case that lessons from some personal experience or scenario could apply to their leadership goals and challenges. It may be appropriate to talk about those topics, but only within the context of their leadership. Anything beyond that, a coach might advise a client to seek a different sort of help, but always stays zeroed in on the coachee's central goals.

And even with a more commonplace and seemingly work-centric issue like stress, leadership coaching might end up helping, but it does so from the perspective of it's part of a leader or aspiring leader's job to manage themselves. The focus is always on their leadership.[2]

Create Lasting Change

One of the reasons we want to stay focused on the central goal or goals of a coaching engagement is that we want it to reach a conclusion. The client does—or should!—too. Coaching is not meant to be an open-ended practice that hooks you for life or for decades. A leader may have a recurring relationship with a given coach, but it should recur at inflection points or crossroads or times when a new "big leap" is in order. It's not a safety blanket.

For the coach, that means addressing the underlying mindset that is tripping up the client and create a lasting change in behavior, not just addressing a specific challenge. Think back to the chapter on horizontal versus vertical development: The rote mastery of new skills is not enough to make a significant and permanent impact on a leadership career. The goal is to develop the capacity to deploy the right skills in the right context.

The goal is to develop the capacity to deploy the right skills in the right context.

To reach that goal, the coach has to do much more than help resolve whatever the current problem is. Instead, they have to change how the coachee is thinking about that problem and or the situation—how the current underlying mindset and perspective are holding the coachee back. Once you break down those barriers, the leader can achieve more elevated thinking and create a real behavior change out of that new thinking. That behavior tends to stick because the mindset and behavior are aligned.

If you only resolve the short-term problem, without cultivating that long-term shift, then the next time there's a challenge the coachee will just fall back to their old habits, because the underlying structure and thinking didn't change. If you have to keep going back to a coach to resolve every recurrence of a similar problem, that's a sign that something's not working. Creating *lasting* change is the goal.

Boldly Level Up the Leader

A coach should not just be a paid listener. Both sides of the relationship can fall into this trap. Some clients just want an ally on their side (or, again, something more akin to a therapist). And, of course, there are coaches who will accommodate this wish. But in the long run, it's in nobody's best interest. Coaching can't have a real impact unless coaches bring their own observations, experiences, and insights to the interaction.

That's why our coaches are fairly direct. They have every right—and on some level, an obligation—to tell the client, "The way you're talking about this situation doesn't sound right." Or, "You're stuck in some old thinking here, you need to revisit that, or at least challenge it." Or whatever the case may be. Obviously they are not rude about it. And they are not telling the client what to do. What they're doing is helping the leader see what they are not seeing themselves.

The need for this kind of candor has been part of my own coaching practice for years. But as the work world has changed— traditional training has been challenged, and coaching itself has become much more popular and widespread—I think it's become more necessary and, in fact, urgent.

In a sense, this approach was something I developed by paying attention to what my clients really responded to. Sometimes they *thought* they wanted a paid listener and a passive ally, but (since that's not exactly my style) they ultimately realized the value of having another person's lens on things. They wanted to be called out, to have their attention drawn to something they'd missed.

Many coach training programs taught that one of coaching's core premises is that the focus is solely the coachee's agenda. I disagree with that. I actually think the focus needs to be on the coachee's *and* the coach's agenda. And that needs to start right away; it's one of the reasons the first meeting isn't just passive listening. We actually make sure our coaches, after the first session, with the client, have identified the big leap that needs to be taken—and that this is a shared judgment, not just the responsibility of the client.

See Blind Spots—and Peek Around Corners

I want to go a little deeper on the importance of being bold with a coachee. Remember the story I told back in Chapter 3 about the client who had no idea he was basically coming across as a bully and a tyrant to his employees? I could only get him to understand by treating him the way he treated others—I literally told him to sit down and shut up—but ultimately it worked. And he was grateful to get the message.

There's a bigger point here. One of the great benefits of having a coach, particularly one from outside of your company or organization, is that they can see things that you cannot see yourself. It's their job to see those blind spots and name them. This is really, truly a gift.

> *One of the great benefits of having a coach . . . is that they can see things that you cannot see yourself. It's their job to see those blind spots and name them.*

When you work in a company, who is going to tell you about your blind spots? Depending on your level, it can easily be the case that no one will tell you because they don't want you to get mad at them—or the person who will tell you is so upset they do it in a hypercritical way that's easily dismissed. (Plus, maybe you do get mad at that person.) Very rarely will someone you consider a legitimate colleague say, "I think you're not seeing this thing about yourself, and here's how it's showing up to me." But that's *exactly* what a coach can do.

> *That unique position of the informed but neutral observer can be invaluable not just for revealing blind spots, but for sniffing out opportunities.*

That said, boldness isn't just about critique. That unique position of the informed but neutral observer can be invaluable not just for revealing blind spots, but for sniffing out opportunities and seeing around corners. The client can't always see what's around the next corner; thinking many steps ahead can be a challenge when you're just keeping up with the crises of the moment. But the coach can, for a couple of reasons. One is that they have probably seen related scenarios before with other clients, so maybe they can spot the emerging pattern before the client can. Another is that they're not directly involved, and can more easily step back and get a clear perspective. (It's actually the same perspective that allows a coach to help a new client identify that big-leap starting point that the client would never have come up with on their own.)

A Tai Chi example underscores this point. One of the practice's core insights is that your mind and your body need to be interconnected. But what shows up for everybody, whether they are beginner or advanced, is that sometimes the mind thinks the body is in a certain place—but it isn't. And any reasonable third-party observer can see that this is so.

So basically every class, the teacher will say something like, "Hand at the top of your chest." And we'll all follow that instruction. And then the teacher will say it again, "Hand at the top of your chest." And again. And maybe one more time before saying, "Lori! Hand at the top of your chest!" At which point I (or whoever) will realize my hand is too high or too low. Whoops!

The idea is not to say somebody is "wrong." It's to point out that what your mind is thinking is not connected to what your body is doing—and while you don't realize it yourself, a neutral observer can see it plainly.

That same idea can play out for leaders and aspiring leaders: What you think you're doing and what's actually happening might be two different things. Part of the coach's job is to help you close that gap. One of the most common call outs is when a leader thinks they are "helping" a direct report when really they are getting in that person's way and creating an additional obstacle or challenge.

And there's one step further: The coach should also help leaders close that gap on their own. One of the jobs of a leader is to manage your own perception—to know the impact you're having on other people, and make sure that impact is the impact you want. That's another dimension of negotiating blind spots and seeing around corners in which a coach is in a unique position to help.

You're Not a Coach Until You've Been "Fired"

Serving as a neutral party who can say the things that no one else can say might sound like something anyone could do. It's not. It takes experience, training, judgment, and patience. And sometimes, it takes a thick skin. At Sounding Board, we joke that you're not really a seasoned coach until you've been "fired" by a coachee.

In truth, of course, that's very rare—but some clients *do* get upset and flirt with ending the relationship as if they were dealing with a rebellious subordinate. But at that point the coach just offers a reminder: "Look, I'm just telling you this. I don't have any vested interest. I'm telling you because it's in *your* interest. If you don't like it, you can fire me, but that won't actually address the issue." Usually even the most upset clients get it, and engage in a real discussion. And once they get over being upset about whatever they didn't want to hear, they end up being grateful. Because, regardless of their reaction, it's likely there wasn't any other way they could have attained this new perspective.

Of course this all depends on that new perspective being a considered and valuable one. The reason we vet our coaches so stringently and train them so deeply is that we don't want them to be offering perspectives as though they were some kind of indisputable truth. It is just their point of view. Because there's a whole other layer of trust involved when you are going to point out blind spots to people. It goes back to seeking "that third right answer" that I discussed earlier. It's about saying "This is what I'm noticing and seeing and hearing, this is what I'm getting from what you're telling me. Here are my observations."

Often, coaches can't quite do this at first. But it's a skill that can be learned and applied, and it's vital. To be effective, the coach has to have an agenda. Not a personal agenda. But an agenda around their coachee's developmental path. The coach is not an expert on the coachee's job; they are experts in professional development. That agenda drives the engagement.

The alternative—just backing whatever the client thinks they want—can be not only a waste of time but also disastrous. For example, remember that executive I mentioned who wanted to drop a lot of responsibilities, but keep the same salary? Well, he had a coach who was all about supporting his point of view. The coach didn't offer any alternate points of view, didn't challenge the executive's thinking, assumptions, or "strategy."

What he needed, and what we believe coaching clients deserve, especially today, was a more assertive response. "I see why you would want that, and I understand your point of view. Perhaps you also need to consider the company's or your manager's point of view, since they will have to find other ways to distribute the responsibilities you are dropping. How do you think your point of view fits in with those other points of view?"

Is this an easy conversation? Of course not! But there's no reason a company should pay for easy conversations that don't actually help. This coach should probably have set a bolder and less compliant tone before this situation came to a head. Just listening and supporting isn't coaching. It's being a paid friend. And coaching should—and *can*—be so much more than that.

In fact, the real lesson here is about the need for a shift from traditional training methods to truly effective coaching. As I've explained earlier, much of the traditional training thinking was devised, developed, and became entrenched in a work world in which individuals spent decades at a single company, shaping their career entirely in that context. That implies a timeline that just doesn't exist anymore. With organizations and careers moving at a different pace, development has to change to keep up. Coaching is much better suited to this accelerated world, where a career is more likely to play out over a half-dozen organizations, not one.

Organizational Impact

While coaching is more in sync with an accelerated work world than regimented training schemes, that doesn't mean a coaching relationship should simply ignore or minimize the coachee's relationship to a given organization. This is where some coaching approaches get tripped up. Focusing exclusively on the perspective of the coachee is exactly what leads to the paid-friend scenario.

That's why a successful coaching relationship keeps organizational impact front and center.

That's why a successful coaching relationship keeps organizational impact front and center. It's a systems point of view. The coachee is not, after all, operating independently from the organization. They can't be just about enhancing the impact on the individual's career, but must also be about increasing their impact in the organization. That's the proper context.

This makes a big difference in how coaching registers at an organization, which in turn will influence the practice's broader potential and impact. If good coaching and its benefits are becoming increasingly mainstream across all levels of organizational leadership, then organizational impact is crucial; if it's only about benefiting the individual, that's not broad enough.

Perhaps surprisingly, even some organizations haven't quite accepted this yet, and still see coaching as a one-off engagement for specific individuals. Sometimes we have to convince them to take a broader perspective. Yes, part of it is about how individuals manage themselves as leaders or potential leaders. But what really matters is how they are showing up in and for the organization. And those things are not mutually exclusive. In fact, they should be intertwined.

Use Technology to Deepen Coaching Impact

The impact of coaching has, to date, been very difficult to measure. First, in its earlier years, the practice was hidden behind closed doors, shrouded in confidentiality. Later, even as the practice became more widespread and mainstream—and certainly a growing number of leaders had glowing anecdotal assessments of successful coaching engagements—there just wasn't any thought-out system for measuring results.

A few years after starting Sounding Board, we were talking to a large enterprise client and discovered that it had its executives fill out paper surveys related to assessing their development through executive coaching. This sounded interesting, so we wanted to know more. How do they track and compare the results? They started laughing. All the surveys were stored in a bunch of boxes, which nobody looked at. It was, they said, just too onerous to sort through all that paper and try to make sense of it.

Sounding Board had developed its own performance-tracking software for internal purposes, and this became the first instance of us breaking that out into a stand-alone software. We realized that nobody had good technology for really measuring development in a twenty-first-century context, specifically tracking something as nuanced as coaching. It was all subjective or attributed.

To the extent that digital tracking systems existed, they were still built around measuring the old, out-of-date metrics I discussed in the first section of the book. Again, some of those methods still have some value, if placed in proper context. But on their own they fall woefully short. We need to add new metrics, and we need ways to track them over time.

Here's an example. Earlier, I mentioned the Kirkpatrick Model—the evaluation model that the training firm I worked for used to gather feedback about how effective our sessions had been. It has four levels. Basically, "I liked it," "I learned something," "I have actually tried this," and "I got some results from trying this."

Evaluating training and development is a good idea, but the Kirkpatrick Model has been around for decades—training and development options have evolved, with the rise of coaching in particular changing expectations. So maybe this model could use an update. Adding a few levels would bring it more in line with the twenty-first-century work and leadership environment.

For example, if we're operating in the context of an organization, then we need feedback from others besides the trainees or coachees. In particular, because good coaching is centered on developing the capacity to make decisions and take actions in the real world, we want to build on that last and most meaningful category in the Kirkpatrick Model—namely, when you've actually put your coaching to use in your daily work environment.

But now let's add some more layers. Are you using your new skill and capabilities in the appropriate situations? Are they right for the context? And what was the impact? To be truly effective, some of this feedback has to get beyond self-reporting, and involve input from managers, direct reports, and colleagues. That might have been a logistical nightmare in the past (probably resulting in boxes of forms that are too overwhelming to sort through!) but with technology it not only can be managed, it can provide new insights and learning for the organization. We have some of this in place already, but we're just getting started. It's all digital, easily accessible, and the more it scales the more useful it gets.

One of the original challenges around coaching in its earlier years was the absence of real external feedback; the only evaluation came from the client's self-reports. And there have been some efforts to extrapolate (often wildly) from that feedback to demonstrate the impact for the organization. But we believe the real key to gauging the value of development is to gather true organizational feedback. This offers a whole new level of information for the organization and the coachee (and, for that matter, the coach).

Ultimately that same feedback system could be tweaked so that a coach or coachee could *request* very specific feedback and get answers back in a timely way that actually helps turn leadership development into an organically ongoing process. A manager could, for example, reach out to a handful of peers and superiors: "I'm going to be giving a presentation on X. Love to hear what you think afterwards." Or it could be more general: "Hey, direct reports. I've been working with a coach, what have you noticed that's changed?" Building this into a single system makes it easier to execute, and track over time.

That, in turn, makes development strategies much more transparent for the organization to evaluate. If I'm the CFO, am I going to commit thousands of dollars to an expanded coaching program if I only have self-reports from coachees to judge by? Maybe. But what if I can see that, 30% of the employees who are being coached got promoted within a year? Or learn that, those managers being coached have a team retention rate of 90%, compared to 60% for leaders who were not being coached. You start to be able to really see the potential impact for the organization.

This approach is part of what's going to cause coaching to scale in the years ahead—being able to show, with data, that it works, for the individual and for the organization. Thanks in part to creative and informed new digital technologies that will update the old standards and metrics that we've been relying on for decades—I'll detail more examples in the final chapters—we're in the process of creating a whole new era of leader development that is scalable, measurable, and continuous.

Coach: Here are some ideas on how to create lasting change.

1. Define and clarify area needing change or problem needing solving.

2. Consider new ways to frame or think about the area or problem.

3. Choose new thinking/new mindset that you want to try.

4. Identify actions, approaches, and behaviors that fit with the new thinking/mindset.

5. Try out the actions/behaviors.

6. Observe impact/results of new actions/behaviors and adjust or enhance as needed.

7. Desirable impact and results support continued adoption of new mindset and behaviors.

Coach: What's missing from your process?

The Power of Alignment

I'm having so much impact that I'm not getting credit for.

Coach: Maybe it's not the right impact.

Well, I think it is!

Coach: Right—but it's not just up to you.

As a coaching engagement nears its conclusion, everyone involved—the coach, organization, and the coachee—wants to see progress in the development of the coachee's leadership capabilities. The penultimate session, then, is the ideal moment to look back and reflect. It's the time to ask: How do we know development has happened? What development happened?

The underlying question—how do you measure progress?—is one of the interesting challenges that coaching had to contend with from its very beginning. In a broader sense, of course, this is an issue for all forms of leadership development, training, and organizational management in general. The more specific challenge for coaching was that it presented a new and different approach—the effectiveness of which wasn't easily captured by the metrics that had become most familiar to business by the mid-twentieth century. Executives who participated in coaching engagements tended to be enthusiastic about the experience, but that enthusiasm was mostly anecdotal. (Particularly in coaching's early days, some executives didn't really want to disclose that they'd been coached at all.)

So if coaching is at the center of a whole updated and refreshed approach to leadership development, then clearly we need updated and refreshed methods of gauging its effectiveness. And that has to start with an even deeper, underlying shift: What, exactly, should we be measuring? And how can we measure it?

This is a big part of what we've been working on at Sounding Board. And we have some principles that guide not only the way we coach and measure the resulting development but the way we want our company's own management and leadership to function:

- Outcomes, not just actions
- Impact, not just activity
- Progress, not just events

Activity Isn't Enough

Traditionally, and even to this day, what mostly gets measured, and emphasized, is developmental *activity*. Taking a class. Attending a webinar. Reading a certain book. These are all activities that one can do, and that might lead to improved leadership skills and capabilities. And they're easily trackable: You took the class or you didn't. It's binary, so it makes the measurement easy.

What isn't being tracked effectively is actual progress. A developing leader can complete all sorts of activities. But that doesn't say anything about the transfer of that potential learning to someone's daily work life or leadership mindset. Say I want to ice skate; I watch a professional skating competition. Does that mean I have a new skill? Of course not! We don't want to measure activities completed; we want to measure actual progress toward building capabilities over time. So in the skating case, can you get out there and at least stand on the ice? That's where we need to begin.

This reflects a mindset that comes directly from coaching. Because of the direct, bold, thinking-partner relationship between coach and coachee, the coach *knows* that although you've been studying videotaped ice skaters, you've avoided stepping out into the rink because you're scared of falling. Nor have you

> *The coach's job is to get you to the next level of actual impact, achievement, or outcome. It's a relationship that's about results, not activity.*

mastered individual skating maneuvers, or learned to fit them together in a program that flows. The coach's job is to get you to the next level of actual impact, achievement, or outcome. It's a relationship that's about results, not activity.

Activity, in other words, doesn't necessarily equal ability or progress. Certainly every teacher knows this; in the same class, some excel and others fall behind. Coaching tries to identify the things that are helping individuals make progress. The answers will likely vary, but the focus, fundamentally, is on the outcome. By its nature, coaching is less about the activity itself and, more about answering questions such as whether you actually got a successful outcome. Did you lead in a way that others are following?

Key to unlocking the ability to track and measure this more intangible progress is to understand the importance of alignment.

Alignment, Not Uniformity

As we work on developing new systems of performance measurement at Sounding Board, we've been running our own internal tests and pilot programs. One of the most promising experiments involved replacing (or supplementing) the usual and familiar evaluation approaches with what we called "performance alignment conversations." This approach is based on our very successful add-on coaching product called "Facilitated Alignment Meeting," in which the coach, the (coachee) leader, and the coachee's manager discuss coaching goals, progress, and continued development. This meeting happens two or three times during the coaching engagement and is universally loved by all participants. The deep conversation, enhanced honesty and trust, and the resulting alignment between the employees and their managers, create a foundation of communication that lasts well beyond the coaching engagement.

There were a couple of overriding goals in designing the application of Facilitated Alignment Meetings to performance management. One was to make sure our approach wasn't just a look back, but included a forward-looking element. And the other was to acknowledge that, in our view, an employee's performance is a shared responsibility between the employee and their manager.

> *An employee's performance is a shared responsibility between the employee and their manager.*

So we had each employee fill out a self-reflection in three areas: performance, impact, and development. And then we asked for three responses in each of those areas. Under performance, for example, we asked each person to give a percentage answer (*not* a yes/no binary answer) to these prompts:

- I knew what I needed to do to be successful at my job.
- I consistently performed what I knew I needed to do.
- I want to improve my job performance next year.

There were similar sets of evaluation prompts dealing with impact and development.

The key is that we asked their managers to answer the same questions: Did the employee know what they needed to do, were they doing it, did they seem to show a desire to improve? And then the managers met with employees, one-on-one, to discuss the results.

Two really interesting things happened. First, employees were supermotivated by this approach. It created a real opportunity for both sparking and framing useful feedback in the form of a dialogue. We got the feedback like: "Oh my god, this is the most amazing conversation I've ever had with a manager!" Employees felt totally energized.

Second, everyone got into better alignment: Now the employee knew what to do for next year, and so did the manager. Both now understood where the employee was and what their pace of development should be for next year. That was because the measurement system wasn't one-way—the usual method of superiors rating subordinates on some single company-wide scale. That method is about creating a sense of uniformity, with everyone being compared against an identical scale for the sake of fairness and comparison. Instead, we wanted to create a sense of alignment, the feeling that the manager and employee are on the same page, working as a team toward mutually understood outcomes.

> *When we're discussing performance, it's not a divisive process; we are all fundamentally on the same side.*

And we wanted that alignment to include a sense of affiliation—building on that cultivation of community I described in Chapter 8. We're in alignment with each other, and with the organization as a whole, we are part of the same community. When we're discussing performance, it's not a divisive process; we are all fundamentally on the same side.

In particular, we wanted to orient that sense of alignment toward the future. After all, you want your employees to be motivated to do better next year—even if they were stellar this year. You want them to have more impact. And nowadays, you want them to grow. Because if they're not growing, they won't stay with your company or be able to respond to the continually changing environment in which we find ourselves.

This points to the most important alignment of all: mutual growth, collective impact. You can shift focus from the activities you think you need, to achieving the outcomes that you want for your organization.

But you'll notice I haven't said that this will be easy. Getting into alignment takes time and attention.

Mind the Gap

As I explained earlier, our affiliation-alignment pilot project focused on three areas—performance, impact, and development—by way of three questions/prompts for each category (Figure 11.1). It's important to note that we intend this basic system to be customized. Every company and organization will have its own priorities, and its own means of framing them, but I'll share the details around some of the questions we asked that proved particularly valuable. Under the heading of performance, we wanted employees to gauge how true they felt it was "I know what I need to do to be successful in my job." Their manager was given a parallel prompt: "My employees know what they need to do to

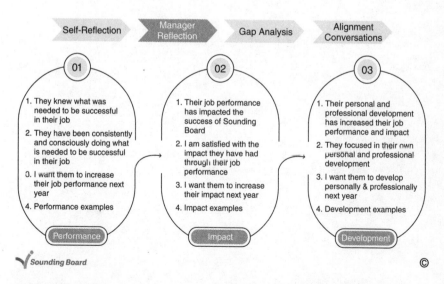

FIGURE 11.1 Example of a manager-reflection questionnaire.

be successful in their jobs." Then, we looked at the gap between those responses. That gap is where we found a lot of very productive information that started a lot of truly productive exchanges.

If employees think they know 100% of what they need to succeed, and the manager thinks employees know 50%, then the employees are probably doing something they shouldn't be doing or not doing something they should. If the employees think they know 50% of what they should be doing, and the manager thinks they know 100%, then there is some kind of miss in communication, understanding, execution or acknowledgment (Figure 11.2). Clearly the employees are not feeling confident or successful. This warrants a conversation about what is causing the disconnect and how to fix it.

The idea is that instead of using a one-way evaluation, you can do a "gap analysis." That means assessing how aligned the manager and the employee are around what the employee should be doing—or how big the gap is between each side's perceptions.

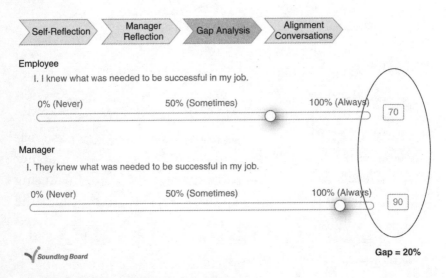

FIGURE 11.2 Example of gap analysis.

That starts a conversation about reaching a common under-standing. It's not just the employee who is responsible for their performance. It is the manager and the employee together who are responsible for the employee's—the team's, the division's, and ultimately the company's—performance.

This joint manager/employee responsibility for employee development has probably always been there, but in the modern work world it can't be ignored or glossed over anymore. We've gone through different waves on this. Way back in the 1950s, 1960s, and 1970s, it was the manager's job (and, by extension, the company's job) to steer workers' career development over the course of basically a lifetime in an organization. Then things shifted, and it became almost fully the individual's job to manage their own career, probably across multiple employers or even across multiple career categories.

We're trying to nudge things toward the center: It's actually a shared responsibility. That's the direction it's really going any-way, but few organizations have really adjusted. Instead of just evaluating the employee, we should be evaluating the relation-ship between the manager and the employee—that is helping the employee, and the organization, be successful.

That's a straightforward enough insight, but one that the tra-ditional evaluation process ignores. After all, when employees leave a company, one of the top reasons they give involves their relationship with their manager. Yet traditional approaches never measure that relationship. They evaluate the individuals as sepa-rate entities instead of as a team of two that have to work together toward success. Why are so many organizations stuck measuring the individual in isolation, when that's not all that influences the individual's impact? Addressing that shortcoming led to the gap analysis.

Already, we're finding that clients *love* this idea because it acknowledges this larger shift in thinking and gives you a very tangible way to look at it. By design, the gap is not just a conversation starter; it's *measurable*. You can see which managers tend to have larger gaps, and work to narrow them; you can look from quarter to quarter, year to year and see if a gap is smaller or larger. It's easier to make visible what's happening. It also helps make visible what *needs* to happen, to change, in the year ahead.

I'll give you an example of how identifying "the gap" might play out, based on a past coaching client. She was an executive at a biotech company—one of the few women on a mostly male leadership team. From day one of our engagement, her perspective was clear: She was not being acknowledged for her impact.

A female executive not being given credit for her impact would not exactly be a shocking development. But I could tell from how she was talking that she didn't actually have the company's point of view. She was basing her idea of impact on her activity, not on the company's strategy.

She happened to be the sort of person who was very task-oriented—always had a whole checklist of activities she made sure to accomplish, checked all the boxes. And sometimes that had an impact. Most employees have to do items on the work list—edit the contract, approve the report, sign on the dotted line, and so on. But sometimes the things on the checklist are not the high-value items. The high-value item is in the unexpected negotiation win, or finding a partner who's going to help the company grow exponentially—stuff that wasn't on the to-do list, because how could it be? It isn't a task. It's an opportunity.

So, yes, she did many tasks. But did those tasks have an impact in the view of others? We had to get her refocused. That started with thinking about how to make her impact more visible, which really can be a challenge for a female in a male-dominated context. But it also entailed seeking better feedback.

It turned out that leadership was mostly aware of what she was doing, the boxes she was checking. And they acknowledged that it had value—but it was not the kind of impact they wanted from a leader at her level. From their perspective, she was doing a lot of work, but that work wasn't moving the needle.

This wasn't an easy thing to hear, but it's the kind of feedback that's vital to getting on the right track. It starts an open conversation about what *would* move the needle.

In this case, however, it took a while for that reality to set in for this coachee. She wasn't interested in thinking about the company's perspective. Instead, she was so upset that she quit and took a job at another company.

But then more or less the same thing happened, and she called me again. I pointed out the pattern: She had just had this same experience, and changing companies wasn't fixing the problem. Maybe *she* needed to change, and listen to her employer's perspective. This time, she got it.

She focused on something she'd been ignoring: What, really, is important from the company's point of view? Not just the frustrated employee's point of view. She learned how to be strategic about this interaction with her employer, and linking her activities to the payoffs her bosses want. She was not just being tactical anymore.

When that conversation happens—about both the company's perspective and the employee's—you can almost see the lightbulbs go on. Now it's possible to get in alignment. And this client did: She was soon doing work that had real impact, and got the promotion she wanted.

Working with Heart

It's easy to understand why an organization might overrely on tracking activities and effort, rather than try to capture outcomes and results. If you have hundreds or thousands of employees, you need scalable systems, and measuring activities has always scaled more easily. But as coaches know—and as that anecdote about the biotech executive illustrates—individuals are just as drawn to activity-tracking. It's clear-cut, unambiguous, like having perfect attendance.

But what does perfect attendance really mean? You can go to every math class, and still fail to master multiplication. It's a reality coaches grapple with routinely: the client who feels they've done all the things they were supposed to do, and can't understand why that's not being rewarded. In short, they equate effort and impact—and that's not how that equation works at the leadership level.

In Tai Chi, we adopt a daily practice. And as we get more advanced, we always talk about practicing with heart. What that really means is practicing with full attention. You can go into your practice and be thinking about your day and what you're having for lunch and whatever else, and you're just doing rote movements, checking the task of practicing off the list. You're not getting the kind of development you would get if you had your consciousness really focused on the outcomes you are trying to achieve. There's a big difference between someone who goes to every class and somebody who truly absorbs what they're being taught—and that partly comes down to how much attention and mindshare you're putting into what you're doing, how present you are to it. Or are you just hurrying through the practice time so you can complete your daily activities?

When I was in college, my roommates always kidded me because I didn't seem to study very much. That was because I not only *went* to every class, I was fully engaged in those classes. I just sponged it up. I paid attention; I took notes. Before a test, I would review my notes and get an A. Meanwhile my roommates would frantically study for days. Their approach was hours of rereading, flashcards, memorization—basically, the standard approach to studying.

The truth is, both methods worked. The takeaway is that there are lots of approaches to an outcome. In the end though, the measurement is on the outcome, not the activity that created the outcome. It is fully possible to study for days and then fail the test. Or not study at all and do the same. Either way, it's the outcome that led us to graduate from college, not how we chose to do the work.

Getting into alignment and focusing on impact helps you see this: It's not just about checking boxes and doing what you're "supposed" to do. It's about understanding what you are doing is really adding up to. In my training days, we distinguished between compliance and commitment. Compliance is completing the designated tasks at their minimum. Commitment is taking every action needed to get the desired result. With increased competition and accelerated change, companies are more successful when employees are committed, not just compliant.

We need to supplement checking task lists with new ways to gauge impact and outcomes— to stay at the level of complexity that the current environment demands.

This is even truer now, in a world in which innovation is so critical to success. When we started measuring activities/tasks back in the last century, it made sense: If I'm tracking tasks on a production line or on a preflight checklist, then the simple answer to whether it was done or not is important. But in the twenty-first century, doing the task is the minimum. Often, a robot can perform a task that can be measured in purely binary way, but you can't use the same form of measurement used back in 1960 when the real jobs of actual human workers have gotten much more complex (even the ones that involve production lines). Now you're trying to measure things that are about new information and thinking—and there isn't a binary measurement for that. Retrofitting today's work world to yesterday's measurement systems just doesn't work. We need to supplement checking task lists with new ways to gauge impact and outcomes—to stay at the level of complexity that the current environment demands.

What Does Your Company Really, Really Want?

As powerful as the lessons of measuring outcomes over activity are for individuals, they may be even more valuable to organizations. In a way, this goes back to one of the core precepts of coaching: Identifying what you really really, want. For any successful organization, the answer is likely to involve outcomes, impacts, and results—not tasks and activities.

Coaching is about changing underlying patterns in individuals to fundamentally improve leadership behavior and decisions.

Coaching is about changing underlying patterns in individuals to fundamentally improve leadership behavior and decisions. Focusing on outcomes and alignment is a way of applying that method on an organizational level.

This doesn't mean completely tearing down existing evaluation systems. At Sounding Board, we recognize that isn't a practical option for an established organization, or even a desirable one. But we do think it's worth encouraging a shift in emphasis, to make sure your evaluation approaches are capturing, enabling, and promoting what you really, really want. Make sure you're gauging the right things, and then adjust your system accordingly to measure them.

That brings us to a final point about our alignment idea, namely, one set of questions focused explicitly on impact. For the employee's self-reflection, we asked: "What am I doing that is impacting the overall success of the company?" And we asked managers to rate and describe that impact, too. This may sound like a company-centric question. And perhaps it is—but maybe not in the way that you think.

Research shows that a key factor in retention is whether people feel that they have a purpose, and that they're actually having an impact. So for starters, this gives the manager a window to see how much impact your employee thinks they're having. Part of what we uncovered by this approach at Sounding Board is that some employees think they're not having an impact, but their managers think they are. Even when they are meeting all the key official benchmarks laid out by whatever performance-measurement system the company uses, employees may not see the larger impact they are having—despite the fact that their managers *do* see that impact. And these days, this disconnect leads to dissatisfaction with work.

Thus, the gap analysis not only revealed useful information but also provided an opportunity to have a positive and constructive conversation, in which managers could spell out what an employee is doing right: here's where you're having impact, here are examples of things you did, ways you behaved that created impact beyond your perception. It's a chance to communicate value, and to identify and do something about employees who might be at risk of leaving because they feel like what they're doing doesn't matter.

It also, of course, is an opportunity to figure out why they feel that way, and make managing changes accordingly. But the most important change is simply finding ways to make this conversation happen in the first place. And if you're just focused on activities and processes, you'll never get there.

There's a flip-side version of this conversation: addressing a different disconnect, in which the employee (like that biotech executive) thinks they're having a much bigger impact than they are.

That opens a harder conversation. But it's a chance to give some very specific feedback. It could be the employee, or aspiring leader, is not having as much impact as they think. Or that the impact they're having is not helpful. Yes, they have something to say at every single meeting, but it's not always useful to the conversation, and they often talk over the other people, for example.

In other words, the conversation is an opportunity to have a kind of interactive calibration, because often employees who feel that their impact is more than it is will end up disgruntled: "I had so much impact, and I didn't get a raise!" That's their honest perspective. But they haven't really thought about, let alone heard, the point of view of their superiors, their peers, customers, vendors, whoever else they deal with.

A coach could walk them through that challenge, but absent a coach, an alignment-oriented system can lead to a conversation that gets them properly recalibrated. They get to see the other person's point of view. And this can and should be a real conversation. "I thought I had a lot more impact than you are naming. How can I have more impact that's visible to you?" This is a much deeper conversation than "Did you do activities X, Y, and Z?" or "Did you meet the list of objectives?"

All this comes out of a coaching approach, and it's not just that I've had many experiences with clients who felt their true impact was being overlooked. We can all fall into the trap of relying too much on the process. It's a challenge not only for companies but also for individuals. I have also spent a lot of time moving valuable leaders beyond their reactions to their performance feedback and ratings, which is something that can create weeks and months of low productivity for companies. The truth is that both employees and companies are ultimately concerned with results. We're in alignment when we focus on the right things together.

Don't Focus on the Problem Outliers

Part of what the alignment approach reveals is instances of *mis*alignment—sometimes drastic ones. As I've explained earlier, this can actually be an opportunity to get back in sync. Remember how I said every teacher knows that you can present the same material to a group of students and know that you'll get a spectrum of results? Something similar will emerge from the alignment exercise. In a few cases, you'll encounter what looks like a total disconnect.

I learned back in the training world, a long time ago, that if you have 30 people in the classroom, it can be really tempting to get distracted by the 1 or 2 who are not paying attention—in other words the problem people. I used to put all my effort on those 1 or 2, to try to engage them. But soon I realized there were 28 other people here who *are* engaged and whom I'm ignoring in my worry about the 2 nonengaged folks. I need to put my attention on the 28!

So in the first break, I would ask those outliers if we could talk outside, and say, "It doesn't seem like this is engaging you, so why don't you just bail and go back to work?" Sometimes they'd object—they signed up for the course!—but I'd politely note that they were not participating, and that was causing a distraction.

About 50% would say: "Oh, I didn't realize! So sorry!" And they would engage. The other 50% of the people would laugh and say, "Oh, thank God, I'm out of here. Nothing against you, I just never wanted to do this class in the first place."

When leadership is dealing with a few individuals who feel overworked, have a completely unrealistic assessment of their own impact, and expect the company to see everything their way, it can be tempting to get hung up on how to deal with those outliers. A company can't prioritize a few individuals when 98% of employees are performing as expected.

I understand how tricky it is. You want to do the right thing, but, to echo the points I made in Chapter 8, if you cross that line too far into the sense of belonging, you're endorsing a false idea of the purpose of the enterprise—which is not to offer a sense of belonging. Rather, it's to work together toward a goal.

While the alignment process is definitely meant to enable personal interactions, it's also intended to offer a bigger picture view. Thanks to digital technology, all the survey questions are gathered and organized, across the company and across time. It doesn't replace one-on-one coaching, but in addition to supplementing coaching, it can offer an organization-level view: Where are we, as a company, in terms of alignment and moving toward bigger impacts in the future? Where are we falling short of that goal? And, most importantly, where should we concentrate our efforts to make the most productive changes?

The Risk (and Why to Take It)

To be clear, our point in pursuing this experiment is not to completely replace or even to critique the existing and perhaps automated structures that companies may have in place. If you have thousands of employees, you need a way to organize the chaos of evaluating and giving feedback to everyone. It's a challenge. However, if you're going to create or evolve that structure, because you need to over time, then it's worth asking: What are the outcomes you want? Answer that question, then shape a structure that leads to that outcome. Too often the thinking is closer to: "We've always done it this way." Sometimes companies are afraid that if they shift that structure everyone is used to, some kind of craziness will ensue. They've got a lot invested in the status quo.

And, really, there may be a kernel of truth in that. You have to create a new structure, then you have to create all the systems around that structure, then you have to roll that structure out and enroll everybody into it. Then you have to measure it over time to see if it's getting you the outcomes that you want. So it really is not easy. Change entails risk.

But it may not be as big a risk as it seems. Chances are, you wouldn't be reading this book if your current approach was delivering all the outcomes you want. You already know, in other words, what's not working. As I pointed out way back in Chapter 2, lots of organizations scrapped performance evaluations in the early 2000s, only to end up reintroducing them— not because they didn't recognize their flaws, but because there didn't seem to be anything else to take their place. So maybe it's worth all that effort to get something that will work better, with more impact.

Making a systematic effort to get in alignment and stay in alignment is a big leap in that direction. It's time to ask, "What's the purpose of a performance evaluation?" It's a time-honored activity, but what is the outcome that you really want to address: disgruntled employees, wasted time, lack of useful information, focusing on the past? Or is it just to compile numbers to rationalize salary decisions? I doubt it. The research suggests very little connection between traditional performance evaluations and promotion decisions. In fact, it's a classic case of focusing on process over outcome, and it's a process that takes up lots of time, money, and effort. The outcome satisfies hardly anyone.

Let's go the other way: What's the outcome you want? And then let's create a process that leads to those outcomes. And let's start by doing it in a way that encourages your managers and your employees to be more aligned.

Coach: Here are some ideas for how to frame and conduct a 1:1 manager/employee alignment conversation:

1. Start with the mindset that both the manager and the employee are responsible for the employee's success.

2. Agree that each should be open to the other's point of view.

3. Create a collaborative context and environment for the conversation—both parties on the same side of the table.

4. Discuss performance, impact, and development, with the employee giving their point of view first.

5. Ask about alignment, but not in a yes-or-no way: "How aligned do you think we are on 0–100% scale?"

6. Discuss how each can work to close the gap in alignment.

7. Name your common understanding before closing the discussion.

8. Have regular alignment conversations.

Coach: How might you enhance your performance conversation based on these or other ideas?

The Big Beyond

> *So what's my next move?*
>
> **Coach: Celebrate!**
>
> *Wait, what am I celebrating?*
>
> **Coach: That you can absolutely figure out your next move by yourself.**

When a successful coaching engagement reaches its conclusion, it's a good time to pause and think back to how it all started.

Partly this is to appreciate the progress that's been made—identifying that big leap you hadn't known you needed, working through all the old thinking you learned to discard, clarifying what you really (really) want, accepting and building on setbacks, reframing your thinking, upleveling your mindset, prioritizing outcomes over processes, and getting comfortable with moving beyond binary frameworks to arrive at solutions you never would have reached before. It's worth celebrating these achievements, and how far you've come. You've come a long way!

But there's another reason to stop and look back: closure, or, as we call it in coaching lingo, completion. The time has come to recognize that the next—the final—step is to truly *own* all you've learned. After all, your coach isn't the leader. You are.

Some clients struggle with this, or at least resist it. They're reluctant to let the relationship go, nervous about losing a "thinking partner" they've relied on, afraid to go forward without their guide. In a way, this reflects a common misunderstanding of how successful coaching should work. Some even seem to suspect the entire goal of coaching is, in some sense, to keep the client for as long as possible.

This misconception—that leadership coaching is about an open-ended, almost therapist-like relationship that could go on for a decade or more—makes some skeptical of the practice.

That's unfortunate. It's true that some coaches and coaching businesses operate this way, and the approach may even be somewhat appropriate for, say, life coaching, but at Sounding Board we feel quite adamantly that that is *not* how leadership coaching should work. It gets too close to the "paid friend" or therapist category; that's not us.

We see a successful coaching engagement as something more like accelerated development, applied in a specific context. When that acceleration period ends, the client should be more than capable of carrying on in that situation, and beyond—way beyond. Yes, some other new scenario might come up (a major promotion, a change to a different kind of organization or business sector), but that would involve a separate engagement that would also, of course, be finite. Although this book reads like a six-month, 12-session coaching engagement, often a shorter or longer time frame is appropriate. For senior and executive leaders, we've found the average timeframe to be a year or a bit more, because the development is more on the capacity building side, and that takes longer. For pre- or early leaders, four to six months is appropriate, as this group of leaders is in the capability-building arena.

> *We see a successful coaching engagement as something more like accelerated development, applied in a specific context.*

Whatever the length of the coaching engagement, some clients do need to be convinced to let go, and I get that. But the ultimate gift of a successful coaching stint is, in fact, that you're not dependent on the coach, you're powerfully centered within yourself. As we'll see in this final chapter, part of the goal is to develop, or simply gain confidence in, your internal leadership compass, so that as you head out to new unknown experiences, you'll sense that compass is true. It doesn't mean you'll always get everything right; no one does. But you are going to be able to make better decisions more quickly, and have a better sense of knowing how to operate as a leader in your organization. The real goal, in other words, should be the opposite of dependence: It's self-reliance.

Building a Leader Success Model

This idea of the internal leadership compass is, in fact, a key element of the leadership development philosophy Sounding Board has embraced—and the development system we have been building to make that philosophy as accessible as possible.

As we discussed back in Chapter 6, traditional "horizontal" leadership training (and training in general) focuses on acquiring skills—but skills are just the start. Bound together, clusters of skills can be thought of as capabilities. And there's another level beyond that; after all, there are plenty of leaders who build up all sorts of capabilities, but who still aren't as successful as they could be.

That next level, cultivated through the "vertical" development approach I described earlier, is what we refer to as *capacity*. Again, building capacity is a distinctly future-oriented practice. It is fundamentally about a leader's ability to discern which skills to deploy, and how to deploy them, in which situations. Put another way, it's about cultivating an ability to deal with the unpredictable. *Capacity is the secret sauce.*

Building capacity is a distinctly future-oriented practice.

Just as we have begun to reinvent the traditional performance review with the nonbinary, inclusive, fresh methodology I described in Chapter 11, we believe capacity can not only be built, but measured and tracked over time. We know this will be a challenge, because so much of it feels internal and intangible.

Yet we also know that there are very real differences between a decent leader and an exceptional one; we just don't have easily legible ways to talk about it.

We know that there are very real differences between a decent leader and an exceptional one; we just don't have easily legible ways to talk about it.

The first step in that process is to break that secret sauce down to its core ingredients. This is no easy task. But it's one that's very much grounded in the coaching idea: The conclusion of a successful coaching engagement is *about* building capacity. It's the culmination of all the thinking (and rethinking) laid out in this book, leaving a leader better prepared for the future. But can that be captured in a way that can be measured and evaluated and improved on a greater scale than one-on-one coaching, but with the same quality and payoff?

After more than 25 years of watching, developing, and coaching leaders and aspiring leaders, I had some firm ideas about what it takes to grow from an average or good leader in to an exceptional leader. The tagline of my 20-year leadership coaching practice was "Transforming Brilliant Scientists and Technologists into Exceptional Leaders," after all. Starting with five capacity areas, the Sounding Board team—including two behavioral scientists—took that core thinking and dove into the research. We found plenty that helped us articulate each component of leadership. But what no one had done is put that into a capacity model that is usable for leader development, so that it could be measured and tracked over time.

So this is our big leap. It's a gasp-inducing challenge, but we believe it can be done. And in fact, we have codified those core capacities that add up to successful leadership. We call them flexibility, velocity, pattern recognition, and self-regulation. Finally, there is a fifth attribute that both flows from

Leadership Capacity = what leaders need in order to lead effectively in highly complex, unpredictable, changing, challenging, diverse, and interdependent/interconnected environment/contex/world.

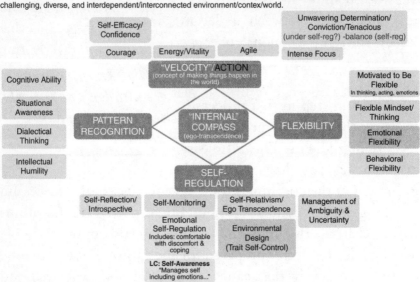

FIGURE 12.1 A model for leadership-capacity building.

and shapes these capacities: the internal compass. These components blend into what we're calling the Leader Success Model (Figure 12.1).

Flexibility (Finding Balance)

The first capacity on our list, flexibility, has multiple components and dimensions—behavioral, emotional, intellectual, even spiritual. One way to gauge it starts with the "social style" model described in the book *People Styles at Work*, by Robert Bolton and Dorothy Grover Bolton.[1] While this draws on research and methods that date back to the 1950.[2] The version that we use internally at Sounding Board, builds on and improves that original thinking, to update it for the modern workplace and to fit with the Dynamic Leader Development approach we are crafting.

What's interesting about that early research is that the original idea was to develop a kind of test that would determine the single best leadership style for a CEO. But what the researchers found wasn't a single best style at all; the best CEOs were the ones who were most versatile. In other words, it wasn't that they possessed some specific style that applied in every situation. Rather, it was that they were able to adjust their style to fit the context. And one key to this was that the best leaders were concerned with finding balance between their own self-interest and concern and that of others—interpersonal flexibility—rather than focusing solely on their own self-interest. In more recent behavioral science research this is sometimes referred to as "ego transcendence." (In everyday language, it means don't be self-serving and arrogant!)

While it's always been important, flexibility is really required in the kind of business environment we're in right now. This original research was way before its time! If you just keep repeating the same approach that worked last time, you're not going to be successful. You have to be flexible to adapt to the context that you're operating in. That could mean adjusting to new competition, or a new economic environment, or it could mean the changed context of moving from one company to another. And an executive leader deals with multiple contexts all the time: from the boardroom, to the executive team, to the all-hands meeting; you have to be flexible enough to operate in different ways in different situations.

A crucial dimension of this is whether a leader is actually *motivated* to be flexible. If the attitude is closer to just a *willingness* to be flexible, it suggests that, deep down, the leader might believe there's one right way to do things (their way), and they don't actually want to see beyond that. They are still stuck on *their* answer, rather than on finding the best answer.

As we'll see later, flexibility actually intertwines with other capacities that entail confidence and even courage. There's a quite interesting book called *The Craft of the Warrior* that includes great chapters on "The Unknown" and "Fear and Fearlessness."[3]

You can meet any challenge that comes your way, not because you know the answer, but because you can adapt.

The concept is basically about learning not to fear the unknown, but to be comfortable with the unknown. Then, you can meet any challenge that comes your way, not because you know the answer, but because you can adapt. As in evolution, the species that adapts is the one that survives.

Velocity (Focused Courage)

What we refer to as velocity, our second core capacity, can be thought of as a combination of courage plus focus. In other words, a leader is able to truly focus on something and have the courage to address it. Unwavering determination, conviction, tenaciousness—these add up to a capacity to make things happen in the world.

Now, I can imagine people reading that and saying, "Well, look, you're either courageous or you're not." So this is a good time to underscore that, actually, everything we're talking about here is trainable. I know this from my experience as a coach, because I've done it with clients. I have also experienced and seen the untrainable trained in my Tai Chi school. We have a great little saying in Tai Chi: "We train what we can see, to train what we can't see." That's why Sounding Board has put so much thought and effort into picking out the pieces that go into these leadership capacities—training those pieces that we can make visible can also train those pieces that don't seem so visible at all.

Courage is a good example. It's about changing a mindset. And in coaching, we regularly have to work on a client's courage for people to even consider making a change. Thus we'll address that from the start: What you really, really want—and what's stopping you from doing it?

The answer usually involves some fear, so then the coaching questions evolve: But really, what's the worst possible thing that you could imagine happening? And then, couldn't you survive that? What's the *best* possible outcome? Do you want this thing enough to take the risk? Then the coach might suggest different scenarios—if X was different, would you do it then? Gradually, we work the client around to take the steps they actually *want* to take. And in the process they end up developing confidence, self-efficacy, and courage. Over time as you do more of it, it becomes natural and you don't even see it as courage anymore (in a good way!) Courage is to act in the face of fear, so, basically, you have worked on the fear or reframed fear so you're not even seeing fear anymore—and now you can just act.

The same is true for the other elements of what we're calling velocity: tenaciousness, agility, focus. By zeroing in on those components—addressing what's causing you to pause, what's making you lose focus—coaching builds internal strength.

Again, when we address the issues we can see, we also address those we can't; these elements are all connected. For example, flexibility is actually quite tied in to the courage and confidence it takes to not feel you have to know in advance what the answer will be. Instead, being present in the moment and allowing the answer to emerge. It's in that present-moment that things happen. That intense focus that comes from 100% presence, and the courage to maintain 100% flexibility is really a very, very powerful combination.

> *That intense focus that comes from 100% presence, and the courage to maintain 100% flexibility is really a very, very powerful combination.*

Pattern Recognition (Beyond Observation)

In a sense, all of these capacities and their components are an accumulation of examples of our third capacity, pattern recognition. As a coach, one of your most vital tools is observational skill: really paying attention to what your client is saying (and not saying) and doing, picking up on the patterns—and the disconnects. (One of my favorite examples is the story I told in Chapter 4, about the client who kept saying he had to "pay the piper"—a pattern he wasn't even aware of, but that by identifying led to a breakthrough that, among other things, made him far more courageous.)

In a leadership context, the capacity for pattern recognition builds in part on a combination of situational awareness and an ability to separate useful signal from distracting noise. But it also encompasses analytical capabilities, including intellectual humility (another way to name ego transcendence because it requires setting aside your own ego). In other words, it combines those observational skills with a certain considered distance and less personalized view that helps make sense of what's been observed, which can be anything from neglected opportunities to misunderstood obstacles. Part of being a skilled observer is seeing through neutral eyes.

We've experimented at Sounding Board with artificial intelligence tools that identify patterns from a client's coaching session. So far, it seems like a potentially useful tool for a coach to use as a supplement—but it's nowhere close now to being a substitute for the insights that the human capacity for pattern recognition, and the ability to integrate multiple patterns, can yield.

Self-Regulation ("Keep Walking!")

Like pattern recognition, the fourth capacity, which we call self-regulation, is partly about observation. But in this case, the observation is introspective; it's about observing and monitoring yourself.

This matters because emotional regulation is really crucial for leaders. The ones who aren't able to regulate their own stress end up putting it back on to their employees—which is one of the basic definitions of a bad boss. He or she transfers that stress to their employees by yelling or making unreasonable demands or lashing out. The more subtle version can show up as micromanaging or as an overcritical approach.

Again, a key part of our current business environment is accepting ambiguity and uncertainty. (This ties back to flexibility, and ego-transcendence.) If you can't manage your stress and end up transferring it to others, you're not going to be able to accept ambiguity—and that's going to limit your potential to lead. Leadership is *about* navigating ambiguity without losing your cool.

And yet not every leader realizes this. In fact, some seem to think practically the opposite—that being noticeably stressed out is a signal of leadership, and if the leader is stressed then maybe everyone else should be, too. They mistakenly think they can use this as a kind of leverage to squeeze efficiency from workers through intimidation and fear. Really, it's having the opposite effect (especially these days, when retention can already be a challenge). Others know that projecting stress is a bad idea, but don't realize—and are surprised to learn—that their stress has become so obvious to everyone else. Visible stress in the leader can undermine the employees' confidence in them.

That said, self-regulation isn't just about what a leader projects; it's about how they actually internally cope with a challenge or an ambiguous scenario. They can learn how to create a pause between the stimulus and the response so that there is time for a breath and choice instead of automatically responding out of

Self-regulation isn't just about what a leader projects; it's about how they actually internally cope with a challenge or an ambiguous scenario.

fight or flight. Many, in my observation, do one of two things: they freeze up, or they fixate on the worst-case scenario.

For those who freeze, all they know is that it's nothing but uncertainty out there and they're not sure what to do. (Workers pick up on this, too.) However stressful the scenario, freezing up is never the answer. I always use this famous line I like: "If it feels like you're walking through hell, *keep walking!*"

Then there's worst-case scenario thinking, which is managing with the primary goal of avoiding the absolute worst outcome. Instead of playing to win, the leader plays to *not* lose. This rarely works. You lose sight of the future you want. You're playing defense instead of exercising tenaciousness, conviction, and determination; you lose your natural flexibility and your natural agility and your natural pattern recognition. That's why self-regulation is so crucial: It's what holds everything together when the situation is really challenging.

Which, as we all know, is practically always.

The Internal Compass ("Central Equilibrium")

This brings us to the final item on our list of capacities. It may be the hardest to measure, but it's at the very center of a coaching engagement. This is the leader's internal compass: In short, making sure all of your thinking, all your behaviors, and all your decisions are coming from an internal sense of alignment. It's measuring from the inside.

In Tai Chi, we call this "central equilibrium." This means that you're not unbalanced by any forces coming at you. Instead, you're able to rebalance constantly, to keep your equilibrium;

you can receive or neutralize an external force, but it doesn't knock you over.

There's a book I really like called *Orbiting the Giant Hairball*, written by a 30-year veteran of Hallmark Cards named Gordon MacKenzie.[4] Originally self-published, it became a cult hit. His idea was that you always stay a bit outside of, and don't get sucked into, the corporate "hairball." You can see everything that's going on, but without losing your point of view by getting caught up in everyone else's hopeless tangle of perspectives and habits and traditions. You see everything, but none of it gets in your way.

I use almost the reverse of that metaphor that gets at the same insight. With coaching clients, I use the term "eye of the storm"—as I discussed in Chapter 3—to describe a version of the idea: You are in the middle of the storm, but you're calm. Yes, all kinds of unpredictable things are swirling all around you. If you lean over too much in any direction, you might be blown over.

But if you stay upright in the center, you keep your equilibrium. You can make choices from being in a centered place. (In fact, the business name I gave my coaching practice was Leading From Center!) Staying in that centered place gives you the more objective, aware view of what's going on. It's the same sense of composure that MacKenzie is getting at, but it's from the inside; and that composure is what gives you a more objective view of all the unpredictable stuff that's swirling around you.

Measuring from the Outside

From my earliest days in coaching, I've been driven by the idea of attaining—or rather, helping clients attain—actual results. From the moment I discovered coaching, I knew I had found my place: focused on new mindsets and corresponding new behaviors that created tangible results.

And part of achieving that goal meant figuring out how to hold myself responsible and accountable. I could tell myself I was doing a great job, and I could simply accept the positive feedback I got from happy clients and know my internal compass was true. But I also wanted some real evaluation from the outside that could validate I was walking my talk—that I was not only balanced on the inside but was also creating tangible results on the outside.

In fact, when I was a decade or so into my coaching practice, I took the unusual step of sending a kind of focus group questionnaire to all my prior clients. I asked them sets of questions related to two broad topics. One dealt with the impact of coaching. I asked things like: What did you learn that you wish you'd known sooner? Or, what's the number-one issue you had as a leader? Or, What development did you achieve that you couldn't have done alone?" Questions designed to elicit a real response, not a yes or no. This brought some interesting responses.

But the second group of questions was even more productive. I asked them to describe both me as a coach and me as a person. Again, this wasn't a check-the-appropriate-box exercise; it was a text format. To my surprise, something like 90% of the people described me as "analytical." I was totally shocked by that, because I don't consider myself to be an analytical thinker as was the case for many of my clients. I consider myself more of a creative, nonlinear thinker, so this was totally at odds with how I would have described myself, and my practice.

So I sent a second request to those folks asking, basically: What do you mean, when you say "analytical"? Many seemed to find this amusing, but they spelled it out for me. "Oh, you're good at observing and identifying the problem, and separating out the pieces of thorny, complex issues. And you're able to go about naming or renaming the problem or stating the challenge in a way that I could think about how to respond to it." Now, I still wouldn't say that's being "analytical," per se, but it was these kinds of coaching skills that gave them the idea that I was analytical; it translated as analytical thinking.

It was a valuable early lesson in making the effort to understand how one is perceived. (And later, I identified a key component of analytical thinking as pattern recognition.) Learning about this perception was something I could never have done on my own, because it was so different from my own perception. This was an assessment that could only come from the outside.

I carried that lesson through my coaching career and into Sounding Board. From the beginning, we were interested in creating our version of a "progress bar," an approach that would allow individuals to track their progress and see their development over time. It was very tempting to do this the way everyone else does—a progress bar of activity. This boils down to "I read this book on listening—now I have listening skills." Or "I took a class on conflict resolution—now I have that skill." I refused to do anything like this, because activity does not necessarily equal acquisition. It might only equal knowledge. I can know what good listening *is*, and yet still have a very difficult time just keeping my mouth shut in a meeting, let alone being a skilled listener.

That's why self-assessment is never enough; you need judgment from without to truly measure progress. Actually, that's exactly what a coach can provide—honest feedback that gives the client a fresh perspective. So naturally we have sought to devise a progress-tracking system driven by that same spirit.

And that involves looking at impact and outcomes, not just activity. Not just "how many books did you read?" but "how many things from those books did you apply? How much of what you learned did you retain over time? What actually had an impact?" Was it the impact you really wanted? I may understand that I should listen more. But in that meeting, when critical topics are in play, am I listening or am I pushing my point of view ad nauseam on everybody else? What do my colleagues, my manager, and my subordinates think? That's how you track progress.

Later, of course, we refined our thinking about vertical development, and the importance of tracking not just skills but capabilities and capacity. And over time we've refined our tracking philosophy further by factoring in the different capacity expectations at different levels of leadership.

All this still requires judgment from without. I might rate myself highly for, say, strategic thinking, and my manager may agree; but if I advance to the next leadership level, my capacity for strategic thinking may be comparatively low for this new context, and require fresh development. This would be a very difficult conclusion to reach simply through traditional self-assessment. That's why the progress tracking that shapes effective leadership development requires outside observation to have real impact.

Self-Reliance

Remembering that outside judgment always matters is key, because achieving that "eye of the storm" state does not mean that from now on you'll always get it right or that you'll never again ask anyone to give you some advice, counsel, and guidance. Context changes. The work world today is different than it was 20 years ago. Your business sector probably is, too. Both will change again in the decades ahead. Your business might get reinvented, new competitors will emerge—and so will new opportunities.

And your personal context may change. In fact, a common scenario among our clients is that a successful coaching engagement results in a promotion. That's great news, but it brings a whole new set of challenges. Sometimes we will continue or start another engagement based on this new environment.

For example, I worked with one client on three separate coaching engagements. That was because his context shifted drastically. His firm's entire business model changed from being completely research-driven, to 100% sales-focused. That drastic shift was ultimately successful, and later it meant the company went from private to public—another whole new world. So I actually worked three cycles with that person, because each of those cycles was so fundamentally different.

But even that relationship concluded. Despite the shifting context, I was always working to make him self-reliant. Coaching doesn't go on forever, and it shouldn't. It should always leave the client *more* self-reliant, less dependent, than before.[5] Another way to think of it is trying to end up more like bamboo than a eucalyptus. Eucalyptus seems very solid—but it has shallow roots. One big gust of wind just takes down the whole tree. Bamboo is both very flexible and has very deep roots. It doesn't matter how strong the wind blows, that bamboo is going to remain grounded.

The Self-Reliant Organization

With that metaphor still in mind it's important to point out here that self-reliance is a quality that should be cultivated not just by individuals, but by organizations. Often, companies tend toward creating dependency, because with dependency comes control. And many companies *think* they want control, but they really don't.

Rather, they want self-reliance because, in the twenty-first century, the best people aren't going to work with any kind of Big Brother looking over them. You don't want employees who feel trapped. You want people who are actively choosing to stay with you. In a world where the kind of single-company career I described earlier in this book is basically just a memory, it's all about employee choice now. As company structure changes, and decisions are made at multiple levels in the organization, you also want self-reliant leaders and employees who have the capacity to make the right decision and progress toward business outcomes regardless of the challenges.

That reality has, in fact, helped shape our thinking about building a leader-success model. This can't be a one-size-fits-all proposition, because every organization has its own set of ideas about what it seeks in a leader. But often, these ideas are never openly stated. It's a question every company should ask: What are the unwritten rules of being a successful leader here? How do we capture those ideas, and how do we share them in a way that's accessible to all? If the organization hasn't identified what capacities and capabilities they want to cultivate in their leaders and actively work to develop and measure these, then a hidden leadership culture can crop up that makes it difficult for employees to advance. That tends to leave out underrepresented groups and leads to a lack of transparency so desired by employees these days. If your organization doesn't have a clear vision of your leadership culture, see the box at the end of this chapter.

Celebrating the Big Beyond

A coaching cycle ends in celebration, for a couple of reasons. You've done the hard work of evolving. You've made big changes both internally and externally and that deserves some acknowledgment. That's why we pause to look back at where things started. You've come a long way from the first sessions. You have the permission, and the conviction, to do something new now. You're ready to head into the big beyond.

The other is, in fact, self-reliance. You've learned to think in a new way, and you're not dependent on or beholden to anyone in order to do that—your coach included. And that spirit carries over into what Sounding Board is creating: We're helping you think differently, we're helping you try some new actions, we're helping you get clear on what you want for your organization.

But in the end, it's up to you.

Early in this book, I explained my frustration with traditional leadership development schemes that purported to identify, say, the five steps everyone should take to succeed. I don't think that prescriptive approach ever worked, but it definitely doesn't work now. The work world is far too dynamic and diverse. One size not only doesn't fit all, it fits practically no one. Not to take the metaphor too far, but there's a reason those traditional strategies end up making you feel awkward, frustrated, uncomfortable, and not good enough: You need an approach that's tailored to you, who you are, how you want to present yourself, how you fit into your organizational context. You need an approach that's customized and personalized specifically for you.

At its best, that's exactly what coaching offers. And that's why we've made it our mission to make a truly impact-driven development system available at a greater scale than even we would have believed possible when we started.

> *We've made it our mission to make a truly impact-driven development system available at a greater scale than even we would have believed possible.*

And the ultimate goal, for individuals and organizations alike, is always self-reliance. And often, in a coaching cycle, the coachee doesn't realize when they've reached that state. With clients, I sometimes use the training-wheel analogy: I know you like this nice shiny bike I've been helping you master, but you don't need me to serve as your training wheels anymore. You're perfectly balanced. You're good to go forward on your own!

The end of a coaching engagement is really the start of a new phase. It might sound scary. But this potential anxiety—"What will I do without my coach?"—is something a good coach addresses directly at the conclusion of a final session. Because the truth is that the whole process has been about self-reliance, not dependence. Now it's the leader's job to shape what comes next, to move forward, to take what they've learned and keep developing and growing, in new circumstances and situations.

This isn't the end. This is just the beginning of a new future created by you.

Coach: Perhaps the model of successful leadership at your company is different. Here are some ways to identify unwritten leadership rules in your organization.

1. Name what top performers do.

2. Observe patterns: how information flows in your organization, power dynamics, who the decision makers and informal leaders are.

3. Look for nonverbal cues/reactions to your or others' behavior.

4. Notice what behaviors your company promotes or tolerates.

5. Ask colleagues for their observations.

6. Find a mentor (more senior leader) who can crack the code with you.

Coach: Which of these might help you learn what leadership success looks like at your company?

Notes

Chapter 2: Letting Go of Outdated Thinking

1. Emma Hinchliffe, "Women CEOs Run More Than 10% of Fortune 500 Companies for the First Time in History," *Fortune*, January 12, 2023, https://fortune.com/2023/01/12/fortune-500-companies-ceos-women-10-percent/.
2. https://www.themyersbriggs.com.
3. https://leaderpotentialgroup.com/why-past-performance-is-not-enough-to-predict-future-success-in-new-position-in-todays-turbulent-economy/.
4. Peter Cappelli and Anna Tavis, "The Performance Management Revolution: The Focus Is Shifting from Accountability to Learning," *Harvard Business Review*, October 2016, https://hbr.org/2016/10/the-performance-management-revolution.
5. "10 Ways to Improve the Performance Management Process," *SAP Insights*, https://www.sap.com/insights/performance-management-process.html.
6. "Employee Tenure in 2022," news release, Bureau of Labor Statistics, September 22, 2022, https://www.bls.gov/news.release/pdf/tenure.pdf.

Chapter 3: What Do You (Really) Want?

1. "Thriving in The New Work-Life World: MetLife's 17th Annual U.S. Employee Benefit Trends Study 2019," https://www.metlife.com/content/dam/metlifecom/us/ebts/pdf/MetLife-Employee-Benefit-Trends-Study-2019.pdf.
2. "Employee Retention Strategies That Work," Qualtrics, https://www.qualtrics.com/experience-management/employee/employee-retention-strategies/.

Chapter 4: Jumping off the Cliff

1. Julie Cameron, *The Artist's Way: A Spiritual Path to Higher Creativity* (Jeremy P. Tarcher, 1992).

Chapter 6: Breakthrough

1. Dede Henley, "Research Says Vertical Development Can Make You a Better Leader," *Forbes*, January 31, 2020, https://www.forbes.com/sites/dedehenley/2020/01/31/vertical-development-can-make-you-a-better-leader-in-todays-world/.
2. "Interweaving Vertical and Horizontal Development: A Whole-Person Approach to Leadership," Sounding Board webinar, August 9, 2022, https://www.soundingboardinc.com/webinar/vertical-horizontal-development/.

Chapter 7: The Third Right Answer

1. Sir Andrew Likierman, "The Elements of Good Judgment: How to Improve Your Decision-Making," *Harvard Business Review*, January–February 2020, https://hbr.org/2020/01/the-elements-of-good-judgment#.

Chapter 8: Making New Choices

1. Julia Rozovsky, "The Five Keys to a Successful Google Team," *Re:Work* (blog), November 17, 2015, https://rework.withgoogle.com/blog/five-keys-to-a-successful-google-team/.

Chapter 10: Lasting Change

1. Amy J. Cuddy, Peter Glick, and Anna Beninger, "The Dynamics of Warmth and Competence Judgments, and Their Outcomes in Organizations," *Research in Organizational Behavior* 31 (2001): 73–98, https://www.sciencedirect.com/science/article/abs/pii/S019130851100013X; Frances Frei and Anne Morriss, "Trust: The Foundation of Leadership," *Leader to Leader* 2021, no. 99 (Winter 2021): 20–25, https://onlinelibrary.wiley.com/doi/10.1002/ltl.20544.

2. Hilary McLellan, ed., *Situated Learning Perspectives* (Educational Technology Publications, 1996); Angela Duckworth and James J. Gross, "Self-Control and Grit: Related but Separable Determinants of Success," *Current Directions in Psychological Science* 23, no. 5 (October 2014): 319–325, https://www.researchgate.net/publication/280771582_Self-Control_and_Grit_Related_but_Separable_Determinants_of_Success.

Chapter 12: The Big Beyond

1. Robert Bolton and Dorothy Grover Bolton, *People Styles at Work: Making Bad Relationships Good and Good Relationships Better* (AMACOM, 1996).
2. "Research: SOCIAL STYLE® & Versatility Technical Report: Documenting the Reliability and Validity of the SOCIAL STYLE Model," TRACOM, https://tracom.com/resources/research-social-style-versatility-technical-report.
3. Robert Spense, *The Craft of the Warrior* (North Atlantic Books, 2005).
4. Gordon MacKenzie, *Orbiting the Giant Hairball: A Corporate Fool's Guide to Surviving with Grace* (Penguin, 1998).
5. Michael D. Collins and Chris J. Jackson, "A Process Model of Self-Regulation and Leadership: How Attentional Resource Capacity and Negative Emotions Influence Constructive and Destructive Leadership," *The Leadership Quarterly* 26, no. 3 (June 2015): 386–401, https://www.sciencedirect.com/science/article/abs/pii/S1048984315000417.

Acknowledgments

In the spirit of celebrating the completion of this book project, I took a look back over the past year. I am not only surprised to have completed this book so quickly but also amazed at the deep level of help and support I have received. I couldn't have done it alone. Other people's input, prompting, challenging, encouraging, listening, and pushing were invaluable in making this happen. I was so supported in the development of this book—my first book—that I can't possibly name everyone. Please know for all the folks who supported me in big and small ways, I am deeply grateful.

A few specific shout-outs . . .

To Rob, my ghostwriter—You are the best writing partner ever and the role model for successful collaboration. Your ability to ask questions that got to the heart of my experience was extraordinary. Mostly I value our partnership, our back and forth, how we kept each other on track. It was such a natural flow and had the arc of a coaching engagement. The experience was more fulfilling and more fun and enlightening than I had imagined. And it's all the more amazing given that we never met in person! I'm looking forward to our next project.

To Christine, my co-founder, and **everyone at Sounding Board**—Thank you for taking on more of the load of running a high-growth start-up while I wrote a book. Everyone told me it couldn't be done—writing a book and running a business at the same time—but we did it in record time, and it wouldn't have happened without all of you. Special thanks to Christine for your support of this project; to Lauren, who took on running the coaching excellence team single-handedly; to Iyad and Pylin, for their stellar behavioral science support; to my coach, Richard, who was brilliant in working me through the process; and to Leah, who handled every little thing so I could focus on this book. It takes a village! So glad we are all in this village together. And a special thanks for letting me try out all the leadership ideas I accumulated over the years and experiment with what worked and didn't at Sounding Board. It wasn't always pretty, but it was always innovative and interesting.

To all my past coaching clients and SB customers—First, a big thank you for showing me how growth happens, what it takes, and what exceptional leadership looks like. Second, for teaching me so much. I can't tell you how many times I have ended a coaching session thinking "I should have paid *them* for that session!" I have been continually awed by the effort, insight, and courage it takes to grow into an exceptional leader. And I am grateful to have known so many exceptional leaders!

To Lenzie, my Tai Chi Chuan teacher—The depth of learning, self-knowledge, and self-cultivation that has come from your school, your teaching, and my practice over 30-plus years cannot be overstated. The experience of power and powerlessness, the depth of presence, and the ability to respond with receptivity and softness are fundamental abilities I don't think I could have learned anywhere else so completely. You have my deepest gratitude for your wisdom and developmental teaching ability. I learned more and was able to apply more than you will ever know.

To the Wiley team—A big thank you for searching me out and putting up with a newbie author who didn't know how the book publishing process worked. I appreciate your belief that I could do it, your patience in working me through the system, and all your work on behalf of this book. You all sparked the idea of this book and carried it through to the end. I can't thank you enough!

To the early years in my career—The groundwork for my developmental thinking was laid in my early career, especially my time at Ridge Training. The depth of daily mutual feedback sessions, immersion in the Social Style model, the sheer numbers of participants and companies I observed, and lifelong friends I made would be the fundamental basis for everything that has emerged since. I cannot say a big enough thank you to all the Boltons and all the Ridgies of the time for this foundational experience.

To my sisters and brothers from my mother and other mothers—Michelle, Linda, Mimi, Lynn, Mary, MaryAnn, Wai, Frumi, Mike, Duffy, and Delaney, thank you for letting me gripe, telling me to take care of myself, having another glass of wine with me, endless calls, walks, meals, Tai Chi sessions, and weekends at the beach. You are my pillars of strength.

To Mike and Lani—Weekly brunches and dinners kept me refreshed, and learning from your points of view has kept me from turning into an old curmudgeon. Love you both.

To Cisco—You kept me sane and grounded, made me play and relax, and kept me laughing and moving forward. You supported me in ways I never expected—from simple texts saying, "You can do it" to going on writing trips with me to taking on the daily cooking. You are my love, my friend, my foundation.

About the Author

Lori Mazan is a distinguished 25-year executive coach who has provided tens of thousands of coaching sessions to execs and CEOs, from Fortune 100 companies to thriving venture-backed startups. Currently, Lori is co-founder, president, and chief coaching officer of Sounding Board Inc., which offers a tech-driven, human-centric approach to leadership development. Her company has delivered over 50,000 coaching sessions to leaders at all levels. Lori is a longtime practitioner and teacher of Tài Chi Chuan and lives in Southern California with her partner, Francisco, her cat, Leo, and her tortuga, Ocean.

Index